GLOBALIZATION AND
AMERICA SINCE 1945

GLOBALIZATION AND AMERICA SINCE 1945

D. CLAYTON BROWN

A Scholarly Resources Inc. Imprint
Wilmington, Delaware

Scholarly Resources Inc.
104 Greenhill Avenue
Wilmington, DE 19805-1897
www.scholarly.com

Library of Congress Cataloging-in-Publication Data

Brown, D. Clayton (Deward Clayton), 1941–
    Globalization and America since 1945 / D. Clayton Brown.
        p. cm.
    Includes bibliographical references and index.
    ISBN 0-8420-5014-0 (alk. paper) — ISBN 0-8420-5015-9 (pbk. :
alk. paper)
        1. United States—Foreign relations—1945–1989. 2. United
States—Foreign relations—1945–1989. 3. United States—Foreign
economic relations. 4. Globalization. 5. World politics—1945–1989.
6. World Politics—1989–   . 7. Civilization, Modern—American
influences. I. Title.
E744.B776 2003
337.73'009'045—dc21

                                                    2003000605

∞ The paper used in this publication meets the minimum requirements of the American National Standard for permanence of paper for
printed library materials, Z39.48, 1984.

To Kay Brown,
Claude Neil, Barney Barnwell,
Woody Brintle, and H. G. Dulaney

ABOUT THE AUTHOR

D. Clayton Brown is professor of history and department chair at Texas Christian University. He specializes in modern U.S. history and focuses his research on economic development. His publications include *Electricity for Rural America: The Fight for the REA*; *Rivers, Rockets, and Readiness: Army Engineers in the Sunbelt*; and articles in scholarly journals.

ACKNOWLEDGMENTS

This brief and fundamental study of a gigantic subject rests on my reading and efforts to digest the publications and observations of many scholars and analysts from a variety of academic and nonacademic fields. It borrows heavily from the works of others, and without their contributions this book would not be possible. Reliance on historians and economists is apparent, but journalists, commentators, and spokespersons of numerous causes related to globalization also contributed to the body of knowledge from which I drew. My sources ranged from highly recognized works to mundane sources of data, from professional analyses to popular literature. Because globalization is a controversial and contemporary subject, the literature was often argumentative, emotional, or adversarial, but emotional diatribes or literature of questionable reliability was avoided, so that the supporting evidence in this account can be regarded as reasonable and accurate. Responsibility for the conceptualization, interpretation, and synthesis rests, however, solely on me.

My colleagues at Texas Christian University (TCU), including Kenneth Stevens, Mark Gilderhus, Lee Woodward, Sara Sohmer, Ben Tillman, Jeff Roet, John Harvey, Todd Kerstetter, Steven Quinn, Don Coerver, and Peter Worthing, shared their thoughts and ideas. From the History Department staff, Brenda Ivey, Stacey Theisen, and Dana Summers, I received valuable help with typing and copying. The staff at TCU's Mary Couts Burnett Library exhibited much patience and forbearance, particularly Brenda Barnes, Delories McGhee, Lynn Sites,

Cheryl Sassman, and Joyce Martindale. Mary Volcansek of the AddRan College and my graduate assistants Carrie Cothrum and Bart Pointer provided support. Richard Hopper of Scholarly Resources furnished encouragement for this publication, and his colleagues Matthew Hershey and Michelle Slavin guided me through each step of producing the manuscript. My son, Richard, provided the perspective of someone involved in the daily business of a transnational corporation, while my daughter, Carolyn, shared her experiences as a global traveler. Above all others, however, I depended on the love and perseverance of my wife, Kay, who repeatedly showed me various sources of information and shared an enthusiasm for globalization. Errors, misjudgments, and faulty analysis are mine alone.

CONTENTS

ACRONYMS

APEC	Asia Pacific Economic Cooperation
ASEAN	Association of South East Asian Nations
ATS	Applications technology satellite
Bt	Biotechnology
CBI	Caribbean Basin Initiative
CIM	Computer-integrated manufacturing
COMECON	Council of Mutual Economic Assistance
ECSC	European Coal and Steel Community
EPA	Environmental Protection Agency
EU	European Union
FBI	Federal Bureau of Investigation
GATT	General Agreement on Tariffs and Trade
Group of 8	United States, United Kingdom, France, Italy, Russia, Japan, Germany, and Canada
ICAO	International Civil Aviation Organization
ICBM	Intercontinental ballistic missile
IIE	Institute of International Education
IMF	International Monetary Fund
INS	Immigration and Naturalization Service
IOC	International Olympic Committee
IPCC	Intergovernmental Panel on Climate Change
IT	Information technology
ITO	International trade organization

IUOTO	International Union for Official Tourism Organizations
MERCOSUR	Mercado Comun del Cono Sur
MFA	Multi-Fiber Agreement
MILNET	Military Network
NAFTA	North American Free Trade Agreement
NASA	National Aeronautics and Space Administration
NASL	North American Soccer League
NCAA	National Collegiate Athletic Association
OPEC	Organization of Petroleum Exporting Countries
PLO	Palestine Liberation Organization
TNC	Transnational corporation
UNITE	Union of Needletrades, Industrial, and Textile Employees
UNRRA	United Nations Relief and Rehabilitation Administration
VER	Voluntary export restraints
WTO	World Tourism Organization
WTO	World Trade Organization

INTRODUCTION

By 2002, *globalization* had become a common word in the United States. It was fashionable to invoke the concept of an integrated world economy into discussions of topics such as foreign policy, economics, world travel, and educational reform. Politicians, media analysts, and academics included the term in their conversations and public statements. It served as the subject of best-selling books and television documentaries. Globalization was, however, more than a topic of intellectual discourse; it had moved into the public arena. Violent demonstrations in opposition to globalization occurred in December 1999 when protestors in Seattle objected to a meeting of the World Trade Organization. In July 2001 a similar demonstration against a meeting of the Group of 8 in Genoa, Italy, left one protestor dead. In February 2002, only a few months after the terrorist destruction of the World Trade Center in 2001, demonstrators clashed with police in protests over a meeting of the World Economic Forum in New York City. Despite its importance in world affairs, globalization remained a widely misunderstood concept.

The definition of globalization is puzzling in spite of the large volume of literature about it. The term began to enter the American vocabulary in the late 1980s as analysts tried to describe the rapidly growing integrated world economy. One of the first printed uses of the word occurred in 1985, but by the early 1990s it frequently appeared in publications.[1] Attempts to provide a precise definition nearly always failed, and one writer stated that "the world might be better off if it had not been used."[2]

The use of the term *globalism* makes the definition of globalization even more slippery. In some cases, globalism is used interchangeably with globalization with no apparent distinction.[3] Globalism may be used to distinguish only one aspect of world integration, such as the establishment of overseas offices by a major corporation, or it may mean the policy and activities of one country in spreading its economic and military hegemony around the world. Since the mid-1990s globalization emerged nonetheless as the dominant word in discussing the economic transactions, migration, and cultural exchanges occurring on a worldwide basis—"the all-too-familiar description," as stated in one study, "for the process of integration and internationalization of economic activities and strategies."[4]

During the period from approximately 1870 to the outbreak of World War I, some elements of globalization were apparent, but economists and historians generally describe the world economy at that time, or at least that of Western Europe and the United States, as being *internationalized* rather than globalized. In other words, some regions of the world had economies with characteristics of global integration. The industrialized countries had begun to search for sources of raw materials and markets for their manufactured products. Surplus crops engendered by the scientific revolution in agriculture brought increased yields and caused a need to find wider markets. Investments in overseas ventures became more feasible as the Industrial Revolution produced surplus capital. Technological improvements in shipping and communications made this internationalization possible. Migration occurred on a large scale; the United States received millions of "New Immigrants" from mostly southern and eastern Europe. And the acquisition of overseas territories by some leading industrial nations encouraged them to establish military bases and trading outposts beyond their borders.

Despite these developments, there is a difference between the internationalization of the world economy prior to World War I and the new era of globalization in the latter twentieth century. In the earlier period private entrepreneurs generally limited their overseas investments to one country, but multinational corporations, or transnationals, had commonly established operations on several continents by the mid-1990s. A century ago governments had greater ability in overseeing the flow of capital across borders and had better control over migration into their countries. In 2002 the United States could not tightly control its borders and governments might be helpless as capital flowed out of their country if investors made a run on their currency. "Perhaps the most striking difference of all is in the human dimension," wrote a prominent scholarly team, "the shift from the very limited international connections for most people of a century ago to today's circumstances, in which a much broader population is internationally connected."[5]

Globalization refers to the process by which nations interact with each other politically, economically, militarily, and culturally, but the interaction is much greater and more complex than globalism or the internationalization of an earlier era. It is often described as an integrated world economy. Speed is a new factor because mass communications and information technology make transactions between countries occur at a bewildering rate. Trade and migration have admittedly always been under way, but the depth of penetration by one country into another, whether economically or culturally, far exceeds the level of earlier years. At the start of the new millennium the term means the surge in international trade, migration, technological innovations, and the growth of transnational corporations, all of which so enhance the exchange of economic goods and cultural practices among nations that borders seem irrelevant. A definite new sense of global awareness is evident in both the developed and developing nations, and the integrated world economy is generally regarded as a positive force encouraging and promoting higher standards of living and spreading the benefits of modernization to most if not all the areas of the world.

Globalization "now shapes virtually everyone's domestic politics, commerce, environment and international relations," wrote one observer.[6] Not everyone agrees that it is beneficial, and they often express their criticism, warning that it causes unemployment and worsens poverty, spoils the environment, and in general brings the undesired effects of greed and exploitation upon the world. "Globalization," as stated by one reporter, "will not lift all boats."[7] Regardless of interpretation, no nation remains totally isolated, because the economies of the world have reached a new level of interdependence.

Studies of globalization generally focus on the economic activities in one country and how they affect people in another. It may be defined as the interconnection of nations' markets, which means the exchange of products, labor, currencies, and many services across national boundaries. When Japanese companies manufacture computer parts and sell them to corporations in the United States where they are assembled and resold to Latin American countries, an internationally integrated series of steps has occurred that falls under the sweeping term of globalization. When a corporation manufactures, advertises, and sells its products in several countries, it is known as a transnational. Transnationals may move their corporate headquarters from country to country and not have a home base. The number of such corporations increased since 1945 until by the end of the twentieth century they were regarded as a principal factor in the development of globalization. Writers cite the Nike Corporation as an example.[8]

The growth during the last half-century of trade blocs formed by sovereign governments and devoted to promoting commerce among themselves enhances the economic interpretation of globalization. Wealthier, or developed, nations are the primary drivers of the world economy, and they have established various bodies for the sake of their own enrichment and for improving the standard of living of poorer nations. The Group of 8, for example, consists of the largest economic powers of the West, while the Association of South East Asian Nations (ASEAN) promotes political and trade cooperation among its nine members that have small economies. Certainly the best known, and most controversial, trade bloc is the World Trade Organization (WTO), established in 1995 to replace the General Agreement on Tariffs and Trade created in 1947. Organizations such as these have a clear purpose: to foster economic growth through cooperation.

A study of globalization must include the role of governments. They arrange and make trade agreements, of course, but they also regulate trade through tariffs and nontariff barriers such as licensing, special taxes, or adjusting currency values. Governments may place special restrictions on food imports if they believe that public health is threatened. A government may impose restrictions on foreign investment and development within its borders in order to protect its environment. Since World War II the United States has encouraged free trade and international economic cooperation, but it has on occasion offended its trading partners by dumping goods on the international market or by stopping imports of particular products in order to satisfy a political constituency.

Another dimension of the role of government concerns its relationship with transnational corporations. Concern has grown over the growth of transnationals that avoid labor and environmental regulations in the United States by relocating manufacturing plants to Third World countries. Critics of transnational corporations allege that they have no national identity because they move their operations from country to country. Other critics warn that governments are losing their ability to manage their own economies to transnationals and urge that steps be taken to ensure the predominance of government.

Technology deserves special attention. There is a widely held assumption that globalization is technologically driven. "Technology is, without a doubt, one of the most important contributory factors underlying the internationalization and globalization of economic activity," asserted one writer.[9]

Technology is only a tool that, despite its importance, must be put to use by entrepreneurs as part of a larger capitalist organization in order to be effective. Technological innovations of the last half-century greatly intensified and accelerated international exchange in a variety of ways. The speedy transfer of massive sums of money across international boundaries, known as capital flow, that occurs as part of a regular business day in world financial markets became feasible only with the development of modern satellite communications. Other recent innovations, including, but not limited to, jet travel and shipping, fostered globalization, and only when these recent accomplishments are used in combination with older ones dating back to the nineteenth century can the full force of technology make possible an integrated world economy. Indeed, international trade occurring on a vast scale depends on the cumulative impact of technology. In this respect both old and new technologies are recognized as having an extraordinarily powerful role in globalization.

Since 1945 the United States has led the world toward globalization not only by its own convictions but also by the circumstances thrust upon it, especially the Cold War and postcolonialism. Near the end of World War II it began to set forth ideas and proposals to reinvigorate world trade when the future looked bleak and little hope appeared on the horizon for millions of people around the globe. The country saw foreign trade as a cornerstone of economic progress for the world as well as for itself and believed it necessary to develop a new order invested in the future with the hopes and dreams of mankind. Opportunity and necessity were apparent for renewed world order, but not the means for achieving it. The United States took nearly a decade to develop its activist policy, but through economic and diplomatic leadership the country commenced an era of expansion that interlinked it with other countries. America's technology and the power of its economy had equal importance in this gargantuan and hegemonic role, so that as the United States steadily interconnected with the world and acquired superpower status, it was the leader in the march toward globalization.

Even though the United States led the way, its own economy and culture were impacted. Technologies developed in other countries affected the U.S. retail market, providing consumers with a wide choice of selections and not uncommonly better quality and craftsmanship. For American industry foreign competition became a painful reality that required bold thinking and innovations to meet it. Certainly the most visible example of the impact was immigration, as a surge of people came to the country seeking new opportunities. American culture became more diverse. Public health dangers arose as the ease and speed of travel made disease readily transmissible.

Migration is one of the principal elements of globalization, and it has special meaning for the United States because the country's history is rooted in immigration. With the renewed migration into the country after World War II, and particularly since 1990, this feature of globalization has become a compelling subject of public interest. America's strong economy attracts immigrants from nearly all areas of the world, with the preponderance coming from Latin America. Many of them enter illegally. Some new arrivals come to escape political upheaval or persecution, but the desire for an improved standard of living stands out as the most important motive. By sheer numbers alone, immigrants exert a great impact, and public services such as schools and health care bear the brunt of this human wave. In some areas, English is used as a second language.

Regardless of motives, the surge of immigrants ranks among the most visible effects of globalization on the United States. In many areas, migrants account for the greatest share of manual and semi-skilled labor. As both producers and consumers, their economic effect is evident, but they also implant into particular locales the characteristics of their culture: food, art, music, dance, and language. Their increasing sense of political awareness provides further evidence of the migrants' impact. Many Americans resent immigrants coming in such large numbers and demand the tightening of our borders, but the human flow across borders stirs ancestral ties and family emotions, which bring proposals for loosening or removing restrictions on immigration. As they embark on the passage to a new life in the United States, the immigrants nonetheless reinforce the adage that America is a land of assimilated cultures.

The Cold War was a central feature in the rising interdependence of the United States and the spread of American culture around the world. At the end of World War II, the traditional powers of Europe were weakened or destroyed and much of Asia lay in ruins. Soviet communism soon began to challenge the military and economic superiority of the United States. The growing uneasiness produced by that pressing situation, along with the widespread belief that the isolationism and appeasement between the World Wars had permitted the rise of fascism and militarism, forced the United States to make a decision in 1945. It had to take the leading role in rebuilding the world or else allow it to slide to the brink of destruction.

American response to communism took two paths: military and economic. Military security had to be maintained, leading to the Pax Americana of the Cold War years that enhanced the hegemony of the United States. The installation and maintenance of military bases and outposts in Europe, Asia, the Pacific, the Middle East, and Latin America required the movement of military and civilian personnel around the world. Because of their exposure as individuals to new cultures, plus the country's heightened awareness of international affairs wrought by its role as the guardian of democracy, the American people steadily developed a broader perspective. America's role as hegemon intensified the spread of its customs, mores, and language across borders and oceans. America's commitment with its follow-up activities in the name of the Cold War—a strategy for defending itself and its allies from future foreign threats, a particularly compelling circumstance in view of the Pearl Harbor attack and the rise of nuclear armaments—was globalization in its embryonic form. All the processes involved in competing against communism—diplomatic initiatives, military posturing, or foreign aid—gave the United States a global presence and forced it to become interconnected with other countries.

The United States also attacked communism through trade. There was a general conviction that as the nation promoted its own economic institutions and practices, it should provide aid to other countries in order to improve their standard of living. For developing countries, generally categorized as the Third World, the United States thought it should further the growth of open markets. No better weapon to fight communism was available, so the reasoning went, than to demonstrate the advantages of trade and commerce. To carry out this goal, the United States became the driving force in organizations such as the World Bank and International Monetary Fund, and it arranged or supported trade alliances. The democratic countries attributed the fall of Soviet communism in 1991 not to military inferiority but to its inability to keep pace with the capitalist economies.

The juxtaposition of Cold War initiatives with efforts to promote economic self-interest through trade alliances set the United States on a path toward world integration as well as encouraging the same in other countries. To be sure, the United States was not solely responsible for the new global economy apparent by the 1990s, but its self-anointed role as peacekeeper and defender of capitalism starting in 1945 made it the principal instigator. Technological innovations and business ventures for advancing globalization were important, but they are too often explored as the sole benefactors of integration because of their immediate and visible impact when, in a broader context, the steps taken over a long period of time by the United States on behalf of the Cold War—whether military, diplomatic, or economic—were also responsible for the interdependent global economy.

Toward the end of the twentieth century as the world's economies became integrated on an unprecedented level, and services and goods flowed across seemingly invisible national borders, globalization became controversial. Strong objections arose and outbreaks of violence occurred. In 1999 about 50,000 demonstrators marched through Seattle to protest a meeting of the World Trade Organization. So disruptive were they that the WTO delegates cut short their meeting and left, with little progress made on their agenda. The Seattle protestors received much media coverage and made globalization more than a subject of interest among economists and policymakers. It acquired a new significance and became the target of further, though less spectacular, protests at meetings of the World Bank and International Monetary Fund.

Critics of globalization have a lengthy list of concerns: the environment, labor and human rights, public health, and even the loss of national sovereignty to transnational corporations. Proponents of free trade and an integrated world economy fear a renewed interest in protectionism, the erection of tariffs and other barriers to retard or greatly reduce the flow of commerce. Globalization stirred public outrage and much serious concern among policymakers, but the benefits generally outweighed the detriments. For those people caught in the grip of global competition, however, the pain was real.

The processes and factors setting off globalization at the end of World War II were rooted in the immediate past. The war was the capstone of a horrific generation of death and despair, loss of human rights, and genuine threats to civilized life, and this experience burned into the psyche of the Western allies and drove their thinkers and policymakers after 1945. For the next fifty years this experience cast a shadow over U.S. economic, industrial, and political leaders, who along with the general public turned away from the carefree attitude of the 1920s and despair of the 1930s and rejected the orthodoxy of protectionism and isolationism. With a renewed work ethic and a determination to achieve a more abundant life, the United States embraced trade and involvement in world affairs as the pathway to a secure and prosperous future. Within this large context, the United States fought over its own domestic issues, including the end of racial segregation, but kept its economy committed to growth and an ever-expanding world trade.

NOTES

1. Jan Currie and George Subotzky, "Alternative Responses to Globalization from European and South African Universities," in *Globalization and Education: Integration and Contestation across Cultures*, ed. Nelly P. Stromquist and Karen Monkman (Lanham, MD: Rowman and Littlefield, 2000), 125.
2. Fred Halliday, *The World at 2000: Perils and Promises* (Houndmills, Eng.: Palgrave, 2001), 60–61.
3. Richard Pells, *Not Like Us: How Europeans Have Loved, Hated, and Transformed American Culture since World War II* (New York: Basic Books, 1997), 325–34.
4. Daniel Yergin and Joseph Stanislaw, *The Commanding Heights: The Battle between Government and the Marketplace That Is Remaking the Modern World* (New York: Simon and Schuster, 1998), 14.
5. Daniel Yergin and Joseph Stanislaw, *The Commanding Heights: The Battle for the World Economy* (New York: Simon and Schuster, 1998; Touchstone Books, 2002), 386.
6. Thomas L. Friedman, *The Lexus and the Olive Tree* (New York: Anchor Books, 2000), xx.
7. *New York Times*, December 18, 2000.
8. Walter LaFeber, *Michael Jordan and the New Global Capitalism* (New York: W. W. Norton, 1999).
9. Peter Dicken, *Global Shift: Transforming the World Economy* (New York: Guilford Press, 1998), 145.

1 | The Cold War

In 1945 the United States took a leadership role in world affairs that set it on a path toward globalization. World War II had destroyed the Axis powers and devastated America's allies. It left the United States as the single greatest military and economic power, and Americans realized they would have to exercise leadership in order to protect their interests and to reestablish the economies of the world. The Japanese attack on Pearl Harbor had demonstrated the vulnerability of the nation, and even though the United States had a monopoly on nuclear power in 1945, it was expected that other nations would develop nuclear weapons, too. Americans believed that they had learned a lesson from the past generation, the period between 1918 and 1941, that isolationism and lack of preparedness had encouraged the rise of fascism and militarism, which led to war. Common sense and the lessons of the past demanded that the country take a leading role in world affairs.

This sense of history in 1945 included more than recognizing the need for world leadership. America's own ideals as well as the practical circumstances of world events came together and dictated a global role for the country. Since its early history, the United States, according to one writer, had felt a sense of mission "to make the world a better place."[1] The Puritans' intent in 1630 to serve as a beacon of spiritual light—a "City Upon a Hill"—expressed a desire to be an example of purity and righteousness for the world to see. The popular idea of Manifest Destiny during the nineteenth century denoted the American sense of destiny to extend its culture and values westward across the continent. Indeed, the growth of imperialism in the latter nineteenth century rested on the belief in an alleged superior culture and way of life. In 1917, when President Woodrow Wilson called for U.S. entry into the World War, he asserted a missionary zeal to extend

American values around the world in his famous phrase, "to make the world safe for democracy." These expressions of mission and goal were schoolbook history in U.S. culture, but in the generation after World War I the sense of mission went out of fashion.

Known as the Age of Disillusionment, the 1920s brought a feeling of apathy toward foreign affairs as Americans focused on the glitz and glamour of the Jazz Age. Consumerism and self-satisfaction overpowered the traditional values of sacrifice and mission. Reform became unpopular and the idea of expending energy, time, and resources for the sake of other peoples had little support. This general social pattern of behavior affected America's view on world leadership and brought a retreat from global commitments.

The economic hardship of the 1930s drove Americans deeper into their introspective mood. Seeing little promise for a rosy future, they focused on personal misfortune and recovery. If anything, the country became less concerned about foreign affairs. During World War II, however, the conviction grew in America that its values of democracy, economic development, and spiritual guidance should be extended beyond its borders. Prior to U.S. entry into the war, President Franklin D. Roosevelt and British Prime Minister Winston Churchill signed the Atlantic Charter, which had broad implications for the role of the United States at the war's end. It included a commitment to protect the territorial rights of other nations, to support the rights of peoples to choose their own form of government, and to back cooperative efforts to improve the economic position and social security for the peoples of the world. It also included a commitment to ease trade restrictions. While the Atlantic Charter focused on the Axis powers, it provided an indication that the United States intended to intervene in world affairs after the war.

Once the United States entered the war, there were more statements calling for leadership. Roosevelt called for the country to win the war and the "peace that follows." Members of Congress expressed their belief that the country must not repeat the mistake of isolating itself, and the Protestant organization Commission to Study the Basis of a Just and Durable Peace denounced isolationism and recommended the creation of a world government. Refusal at the end of World War I to join the League of Nations, a world organization conceived by Wilson, was now regarded as a tragic error, and Americans widely believed that participation on their part might have prevented World War II. Examples of mistakes were plentiful: the refusal to take a stand in the Manchurian crisis of 1931, the refusal to intervene against the fascists in the Spanish Civil War in the 1930s, and the Neutrality Act of 1935 that isolationists pushed through Congress. Now in 1945 the failures to act in these instances were perceived as great blunders, and the country could no longer afford to withdraw from the world. Statements and resolutions clamoring for the United States to take an active role in world affairs became common, and even though there were differences about the nature of the role, there was little doubt that the isolationism in vogue in the 1920s and 1930s was unpopular.[2] This shift in thinking put the United States on a different footing from the previous generation and was part of the ideology that drove the country toward globalization.

A commitment to end isolationism was not enough, however, to propel the United States into active leadership. In 1945 the country also considered its practice of appeasement after World War I to be a mistake. Appeasement and isolationism were not inseparable, but the failure to protest or intervene in several instances was now thought to have encouraged Adolf Hitler and the Japanese militarists. Outstanding examples in this regard were Hitler's reoccupation of the Rhineland in 1936, Benito Mussolini's invasion of Ethiopia in 1936, the Japanese invasion of China in 1937, the lack of a strong reaction to the Japanese bombing of the American ship *Panay* in 1937, Hitler's annexation of Austria in 1938, and the famous Munich Agreement later in 1938. By not taking a firm stand against aggression, Americans thought they had let dictators and tyrants overpower smaller and weaker countries and thereby encouraged them to strike at the United States and its Western allies. It was now imperative to correct this lack of resolve. Such reasoning paralleled the American rejection of isolationism and positioned the country for a global commitment against aggression and violation of human rights.

Leadership had an economic dimension. Like other Western countries, the United States between the wars had practiced "economic protectionism," which was another expression of isolationism. In 1945 the country realized that its use of protective tariffs for the past generation had been a mistake. Fascism had benefited from Germany's economic collapse, which owed much to the reparations imposed by the Allies in 1919. Free trade had to be practiced, particularly since the war against the Axis powers had left the United States as the undisputed military and economic leader of the world. A sense of immediacy about the American economy filled the air, too, because of the fear that the United States would return to the Great Depression with the end of the war. Hence, the urgent anticipation of massive unemployment combined with the larger sense of mission embedded in the American psyche, and the determination to reverse the isolationism and appeasement of the previous generation, placed the United States in a position in 1945 that left no choice: it had to take an active and energetic position in world affairs for its own protection and for the peace and security, both military and economic, of the rest of the world. If a threat to the anticipated new order arose, America should be prepared to rebuke it. This ideology, a popular opinion, was common throughout the country.

Few better examples were available to show the important new sense of mission and history than the U.S. promotion of the United Nations. For the spirit of nationalism emerging during the war, the notion of an international body having the world's powers as members and designed to settle differences and disputes seemed more than logical—it was essential. An indication of that position came from a publicist for the internationalists: "Now for the first time in our lifetime, alone of all generations of Americans, we have it within our power to do what we failed to do in 1919—to atone, in a measure, for the error of judgment which permitted us to witness the anguish, share the suffering and bear the stupendous costs of a second world war."[3]

Roosevelt was a firm believer in a world organization and lobbied for it among the British, Soviets, Chinese, and other countries during the war. Toward the end of World War II, Soviet intransigence was becoming evident and the Cold War was in its embryonic stage, but Roosevelt put great hope in the ability of the organization to encourage and promote world peace and security. In April 1945, shortly after Roosevelt's death, President Harry S. Truman led the American delegation at the San Francisco Conference, the meeting of the founding members of the United Nations. On behalf of the United States, Truman stated: "We must build a new world, a far better world—one in which the eternal dignity of man is respected."[4]

Whether the United Nations proved to be an effective mechanism for the sake of world peace is a matter of opinion. It was beneficial for the United States with respect to the Korean War because the Soviet delegates were boycotting the Security Council and could not block UN action with their veto. President Dwight D. Eisenhower pushed a resolution through the organization that pressured Great Britain and France to withdraw from Egypt during the Suez Crisis of 1956. During the Cuban Missile Crisis of 1962, America's UN ambassador, Adlai Stevenson, denounced Soviet action in Cuba. To an extent, the organization refereed the antagonism between the superpowers and was a shock absorber for other conflicts. Regardless of the merits of the United Nations, the American enthusiasm for it in the early years after the war reflected the country's intention to be involved in world affairs.

No threat to world peace was apparent in 1945, but the relationship between the United States and the Soviet Union steadily deteriorated, until by 1947 the Truman administration took action to counter Soviet influence. During these two years, America's Cold War ideology was based on a determination not to practice appeasement or abandon the sense of mission. George Kennan, U.S. ambassador to the Soviet Union, organized and wrote much of the rationale for fighting the Cold War. In a series of articles and reports he expressed the growing belief that the Soviet Union had a goal of world conquest and that the United States must be prepared to defend liberty and freedom on a global level.

Kennan firmly believed the Soviets would not accept coexistence with the capitalist countries, and since the Soviet Union's goals were revolutionary and global, only strong and determined resistance by the West would prevent its encroachment on other peoples. Kennan saw a parallel with the 1930s, when fascists used aggression to swallow up territory, and he thought the appeasement practiced by the West had only placated Hitler temporarily. Kennan did not want history to repeat itself. To avoid war, he urged, the United States should try to contain Soviet influence. Inherent in Kennan's rationale, and indeed that of postwar America, was a commitment to combat Soviet aggression around the world by deploying a strategy of military and economic assistance on an unprecedented level.

The instigation of the Truman Doctrine and the Marshall Plan was the first major extension of the new postwar ideology of mission aimed directly at communism. Although U.S. policymakers gave no thought to globalization at the time, these highly successful programs of foreign aid nonetheless strengthened and reinforced the ties between the United States and Western Europe. The Marshall Plan in particular laid the foundation for further action by the United States to link itself economically as well as diplomatically to other governments around the world.

Historians debate the origin of the Cold War and the extent to which the United States was responsible, but President Truman saw the Soviet Union as a threat to world security and believed it sought to extend Communist ideology and practice espionage on a global scale. American strategists felt compelled to fight back on an equally broad scale, so from its beginning the Cold War was waged on a world basis. Herein lay the connection of the superpower struggle with the onset of globalization. Driven by its determination not to let oppressive powers run amok, the United States cast itself in the role of the world's peacekeeper and consciously sought to use trade, diplomacy, foreign aid, and military power in any area where communism posed a threat. This was a reversal of the past forced upon the country by Soviet aggrandizement.

In 1947 the United States faced its first Communist challenge with the crisis over Greece and Turkey. During the previous year the Soviet Union had demanded that Turkey relinquish its authority over the Dardanelles, the strait that had come under Turkish control in 1936. Russian ships had to pass through the Dardanelles to reach the sea, and Soviet leader Joseph Stalin resented Turkey's jurisdiction. The Truman administration saw Stalin's pressure on Turkey as an effort to expand Soviet influence, and in 1947, when Communist guerrillas participated in a civil war against the Greek government, the United States judged the two incidents to be a Soviet-related subterfuge. Truman wanted to stand up to the Soviet threat, and with the help of Congress he provided American financial aid and civilian personnel to assist the Turkish and Greek governments. "I believe," he said, "that it must be the policy of the United States to support free people who are resisting attempted subjugation by armed minorities or by outside interests."[5] From the perspective of the United States, the Soviets had initiated a threat, which required resistance, to stability in the Mediterranean. The decision to commit resources in this instance became known as the Truman Doctrine, but in a broader sense it was the beginning of the U.S. fight against the perceived global Communist threat as well as the first instance of U.S. policy and action after World War II that was organized and carried out in a global manner.

It was the Marshall Plan, however, that firmly established the intention of the United States to oppose communism. It was also the clearest signal of the new American policy to be a world leader. Previous aid packages to Europe through the United Nations Relief and Rehabilitation Administration (UNRRA) were made unilaterally and mostly to Britain and France, but economic conditions had worsened throughout Europe, with food shortages being the most dangerous.

The fear that internal disruption and communism would grow under such chaotic conditions spread by 1947. Italy, France, and occupied West Germany appeared to be the most vulnerable. In June 1947, Secretary of State George Marshall announced the plan, which eventually provided nearly $12 billion to the European recipients. This was a staggering amount for the time and served as the catalyst for rebuilding Western Europe, which soon figured prominently in global trade. And even though the plan excluded no country in Europe, its massive assistance was meant to counter Soviet influence. Luckily the Soviets refused the aid and would not allow it for those countries under its dominance.

The Marshall Plan was a dramatic setback for the isolationists and eased the path for the United States to become a global power broker. So successful was the plan that it is credited with the revitalization of Western Europe after World War II and the repression of communism there. It renewed America's economic ties with Europe, and through the experience the United States discovered the effectiveness of foreign aid in the Cold War. Through the plan the Truman administration also sought to persuade Europeans to adopt American business practices and to model their economy along "quintessentially American" mores. "In effect, the Marshall Planners," claimed one historian, "functioned as evangelists on behalf of the American way."[6] Europeans resented and resisted these efforts to remake their culture, but the plan, if nothing else, gave the United States its own aggrandizement on the Continent. This critical step in the postwar period could arguably be regarded as the first step by the United States in becoming a global power.

Closely on the heels of the announcement of the Marshall Plan came other events that solidified the position of the United States as the defender of the Free World. Questions quickly arose over the joint occupation of Germany by Allied and Soviet forces and led to their first direct confrontation with one another. In 1948, Stalin shut down the Allied highway that gave access to West Berlin, threatening the city. Truman insisted on maintaining West Berlin as a symbol of Western democracy and had the U.S. Air Force supply the city by air. Known as the Berlin Airlift, this dramatic gesture of America's refusal to be intimidated thrust the country into the face of Stalinist Russia. Neither side wanted war, however, and when Stalin lifted his blockade of West Berlin in 1949, each superpower had demonstrated its resolve not be bullied and also its willingness to avoid war. From the standpoint of the United States, the Soviet Union was a formidable opponent that could be expected to act aggressively and persistently in its goal of expanding communism.

In a psychological sense the Berlin Airlift broadened Americans' awareness of international events. News coverage of cargo planes flying into Berlin in order to keep West Berliners supplied with food, clothing, and other necessities put the Cold War into a visual context. Americans could easily grasp the confrontation with the Soviet Union as they saw newsreels and photographs of aircraft flying into Berlin, sometimes arriving as often as one plane every ninety seconds. In 1949 the U.S. Air Force staged a nonstop flight of a B-36 bomber around the world in order to demonstrate the capability of American military power. Done partly to intimidate the Soviets, it dramatically demonstrated the global nature of the Cold War and the extension of U.S. defenses. These two events, each being a technological and logistical accomplishment, clearly expressed the struggle of the United States against communism in spectacular terms. Such action taken in the name of world peace resonated throughout the American people and forced them to be acutely aware of global events.

One example of the new U.S. global strategy wrought by the Cold War was the creation of the North Atlantic Treaty Organization (NATO) in 1949. America's European allies strongly feared a renewal of war by the Soviet Union and wanted assurances from the United States that it would not hesitate to join in such a war. Their need for assurances came from the fact that the United States had waited for about two years before entering into both World Wars. Truman's policy of containment fit well with the European desire for a commitment, so negotiations, which began in 1948, bore fruit in 1949 when the United States joined eleven nations of Western Europe in promising to come to each other's aid in case of war. NATO was aimed deliberately at the Soviet Union and represented a dramatic shift from the long-established position taken by the United States to avoid entanglement in foreign affairs. It was a clear signal the country intended to follow a new internationalist foreign policy.

Although events in Europe captured the attention of the press and most Americans, there were developments in less-known areas that created uneasiness over the growth of communism. In 1945 the traditional imperial powers of Europe began withdrawing from their colonial empires due either to popular uprisings or to their inability to maintain control. India gained its independence from Britain in 1947, and Ceylon and Burma in 1948. In 1949 the Netherlands withdrew from the Dutch East Indies after 300 years of rule. France lost Indochina in 1954 to the Communist movement led by Ho Chi Minh.

In the course of the Cold War, this development, known as postcolonialism, became one of the major considerations of U.S. foreign policy. The decline of European imperialism removed the steadying influence of Western culture in various parts of the world, thus creating a power vacuum with military and economic repercussions for the United States. Forces of nationalism were emerging with renewed vigor, and people long subjected to colonial rule wished to declare their emancipation. To prevent the influx of communism into the former colonies, the United States had to assume the role of guardian and protector. It did not want to appear as clinging too closely to reactionary or regressive regimes, but it wanted to encourage newly liberated peoples to erect democratic governments, and it hoped to establish its influence as a trading partner in order to keep the former colonies operating open markets. In still another respect, therefore, the United States faced a historic shift of power at a world level and felt compelled to view its own security and well-being in global terms.

Communists participated in and in some cases led guerrillas in attacking the imperial powers, but not all uprisings were Soviet inspired or led. There were often conflicts between social classes or ethnic groups. To an extent the United States had had a similar experience with the Philippines, though much earlier. Uprisings for independence attracted sympathy in the United States, but the changes were nonetheless unsettling because of the monolithic interpretation of communism as a worldwide effort coordinated in Moscow. The fall of colonial governments, which in some cases had existed for centuries, and their rapid replacement by friendly or unfriendly factions elevated apprehension and uncertainty over the shifting of power in the world.

For the United States, 1949 proved to be an eventful year as it forged a global foreign policy. In that year Communist leader Mao Zedong succeeded in seizing control of China, and the Soviet Union exploded its first nuclear bomb. These two developments widened the threat of communism to Asia and greatly escalated the danger of confrontation. Red China's vast resources of manpower made it a dangerous foe, and the possession of nuclear weapons by the leading Communist power raised the probability that the United States would be attacked in a major war. Such frightening conditions made it essential to exert every possible effort to thwart communism and protect U.S.

rights in Asia as well as in Europe. Gone were the advantages of the British and French maintaining their empires there, and gone were the geographic advantages of living an ocean away—across the Pacific—from warring powers. Nuclear weapons and the advances in air power made the surprise attack at Pearl Harbor seem outdated and mild in comparison.

Even though the United States avoided a nuclear war, it bogged down in a land war with Red China in Korea that started in 1950. The fighting seesawed up and down the Korean peninsula until the Chinese intervened in 1950 and drove the United States back to a position generally along the 38th parallel. A stalemate developed as Truman concluded that the conflict would have to be a "limited war" and the Chinese wanted to not deepen the conflict. Truman's successor, President Eisenhower, ended the war with an armistice agreement in 1953, which left each side occupying roughly the same area it had held in the beginning.

The global nature of American economic, diplomatic, and cultural activities had reached a new threshold by the end of the Korean War due to the new alignment of power from the conditions of 1945. Russia had solidified its grip on its East European satellites, which posed a threat to the rest of the Continent. China was Communist and had indicated through its intervention in Korea that it would fight. Uprisings in other parts of the world, whether inspired or supported by the Soviets, made clear the global appeal of Marxism to peoples eager to overthrow colonial rulers and to establish their own national identities. Communists stood ready to fill the power vacuums left by European colonial powers, a growing development around the world that put the United States in the difficult position of fighting the spread of communism while assisting countries in their efforts to form new governments based on self-rule. The United States had stood firm on both sides of the world through economic aid, military alliances, and war. It now found itself in a position of leadership that it had never experienced: it was extended militarily around the globe, with soldiers and sailors stationed in numerous bases and ports. In the words of one writer, "Truman had defined American policy for the next generation."[7]

The Cold War had a cultural effect on military and civilian personnel similar to a regular war in regard to international travel and transcultural exposure. Wartime service extends the travel experience of military personnel, and they are likely to have a new perspective and a greater awareness of the different societies they encounter. The same was true throughout the Cold War, and the fact that several million Americans were stationed at overseas bases, whether in the armed forces for a career or for a limited term, encouraged a broader understanding of the world among the general American population.

An unexpected event occurred in October 1957 that brought home the impact of the Cold War to American citizens. That month the Soviet Union launched Sputnik, the first Earth-orbiting satellite. It came as a surprise that a Communist nation led in space exploration, and Sputnik had serious security ramifications because it demonstrated the strong thrust of Soviet rockets. Such rockets enabled the Soviets to strike at cities in the Western Hemisphere. No longer could the United States regard the edge of the sea as its line of defense, nor could it look upon the territory of its allies as the point of battle. America's oceanic isolationism forever disappeared with Sputnik. For the first time the United States now resembled other nations that had not benefited from the advantage of geographic protection; it lived with the possibility of instant nuclear attack. This unwelcome development forced Americans to think globally, to realize how their own personal security related to events literally on the other side of the Earth. Sputnik's demonstration of the Soviets' rocket capability had erased their line of defense. As stated by one observer, "the intercontinental [ballistic] missile [ICBM] has annihilated the protection of the oceans."[8]

The importance of the ICBM in removing the traditional geographic isolation of the United States received a frightening reinforcement with the Cuban Missile Crisis of 1962. That incident brought the superpowers to their most serious confrontation throughout the Cold War, one in which Americans faced the real possibility of seeing their cities undergo the same fate as Hiroshima and Nagasaki. At issue was the attempt by the Soviet Union to place ICBMs in Cuba, a move considered unacceptable to the United States. President John F. Kennedy ordered a naval blockade of Soviet ships en route to Cuba and placed America's armed forces on alert. For three days the country braced for the worst, sleeping uneasily as it waited for an attack from a regime on the other side of the planet. Thanks to both American and Soviet leadership, the crisis was averted and the world sighed with relief, but the incident left no question that each citizen now lived under the threat of atomic attack. Spurred by the Cold War, this new technology, combining atomic energy with a missile launched from far away, made strikingly clear the vulnerability of the United States, a new reality in American life only with the recent accomplishments in the technology of warfare. War had become instantaneous, and the ICBM was the weapon of the global age. If for no other reason, survival in this era of immediacy required a knowledge and awareness, with protective measures, too, of the crosscurrents of international intrigue and the readiness to deploy military forces to any spot. From this perspective of the Cold War, globalization was a matter of life and death.

Rocketry and satellites heightened global awareness in still another manner: they demonstrated that Earth was part of a planetary system, a mass truly orbiting in space. Regardless of man's intellectual awareness of Earth as a planet, the fact that a satellite was circling some 150 miles beyond Earth's atmosphere impacted the primitive psyche of people. Sputnik and the first satellites left no question that, regardless of our ideologies and cultures, humankind lived a common life on a single planet.

In an immediate sense, Sputnik was responsible for the passage of the National Defense Education Act in 1958. With the Soviet achievement, the United States feared that it was losing the technological race, and there was a common belief that unless the country improved its educational system, the Soviet Union could be expected to attain technical and engineering superiority in a relatively short while. Such superiority would endanger the United States, so action had to be taken to increase the production of scientists and engineers. President Eisenhower urged such an undertaking in his first press conference after the launching of Sputnik, and Congress quickly responded with the National Defense Education Act. This measure, providing federal funding for research and educational programs, was only one result of the sense of global insecurity wrought by the Russian breakthrough into space. As one historian explained, "Americans questioned their achievements, their educational system, and their values" when Sputnik began circling Earth.[9]

Because of the inauguration of the space race initiated by Sputnik, the United States accelerated its research and development of defense and related technologies. Some of the innovations that resulted from this "Cold War research" enhanced and intensified globalization. Communications satellites were the most obvious example because they pioneered the global communications systems that became commonplace in the latter twentieth century. The first voice transmission from outer space came in December 1958 with a prerecorded Christmas message from President Eisenhower sent from an Atlas missile. The National Aeronautics and Space Administration (NASA) launched an applications technology satellite (ATS) in 1966 that provided the first full-disk photography of Earth, a feat regarded as a historic milestone. Fifteen years later the ATS provided countries in the Pacific with a communications link for medical emergencies and classroom instruction. In 1974 the first commercial communications satellite was Western Union's Westar I, which furnished video, facsimile, data, and voice communication service. In 1975 the RCA satellite Satcom provided the fifty states of the Union with television coverage and voice communication service. Soon other countries launched communications satellites: Indonesia in 1976, Japan in 1978, India in 1982, and Australia in 1985. These early developments that had originated in the Cold War race with the Soviet Union eventually led to peaceful uses of space. It was primarily the latter that enhanced globalization, because the modern integrated world economy depends on the availability of rapid international communications. These technological feats exemplified the Cold War's contribution to the development of globalization.

Probably the best-known example of a Cold War technological spinoff is the Internet. In 1964 the RAND Corporation, described as a Cold War think tank, dealt with the question of maintaining military communications after a nuclear attack. RAND discussed their ideas with the Pentagon and then proposed "a decentralized, blast proof, packet-switching network" with the Massachusetts Institute of Technology (MIT) and the University of California at Los Angeles (UCLA). The Department of Defense, through the Advanced Research Projects Agency, provided funding for development of the proposed network, ARPANET. In 1969, UCLA established the first computer base of the Internet, and soon a few others were also connected. Additional units joined the network, and it grew phenomenally. By 1983, a vast network of computers was linked, and ARPANET left the network and became the Military Network, or MILNET. Other federal agencies and many commercial firms then joined the network, until by the early 1990s, when the Cold War ended, the Internet was established in over forty countries.

The Internet revolutionized the transfer of information around the world. Known generally as the Information Technology Revolution, the use of Internet communications had ramifications for nearly all facets of life. So complex and far-reaching were the implications of the new information revolution that its historical outcome remains undetermined. This technological development also originated in the United States because of the pressure exerted by the fear of nuclear war with the Soviet Union.

Globalization imposed by America's sense of mission reached its high point with the Vietnam War, the largest military operation undertaken by the United States since World War II. At the peak of the fighting, 500,000 soldiers were involved, and nearly 50 percent of the United States' military resources and personnel were linked to the effort. Air strikes were a main factor in the combat strategy of the United States, and the air force and navy together dropped a larger tonnage of bombs in the course of the Vietnam War than they did on Japan and Germany during World War II. More U.S. ground troops were deployed in Vietnam than in Korea.

An important aspect was the use of television in covering the war. Americans at home could watch in their own living rooms the daily operations and combat for the first time in history. Viewers could see the savagery and brutality of war and realize the real-life implications of the global commitment against communism. Americans became more aware of geopolitics through constant news coverage and analyses. Indeed, the geography, politics, and nature of human life in Southeast Asia became familiar to them. This development brought Asia into their dialogue and thoughts on a new scale and thereby broadened the country's Europe-centered outlook to include the Pacific regions of the world. To a point the Korean War had a similar impact, but television sets were not yet found in every household in the early 1950s, so the medium's impact was greater with the Vietnam struggle. War was no longer an activity waged out of sight in remote areas; global communications now made each citizen confront the reality and wisdom of his beliefs.

In another respect the Vietnam War promoted globalization, but with a delayed effect. In his efforts to extricate the United States from the fighting, President Richard Nixon sought to improve Washington's relationship with Communist China. In 1972 he made an official visit to Beijing and along with Chinese officials declared his wish to normalize relations. Each power indicated publicly a desire to reduce international conflict, and each declared it did not seek hegemony in Southeast Asia. At the time these statements amounted only to gestures of goodwill, but in 1978 full diplomatic relations started between the two nations. The United States also lifted its trade embargo against

China, and therein lay one of the benefits of Nixon's diplomatic initiative, which had begun as part of his plan to weaken the ties of North Vietnam with its Communist brethren. China wanted to modernize and develop a "socialist market economy." Indeed, it became one of America's important trading partners and joined the World Trade Organization in 2002. This development, like other facets of globalization, originated as a Cold War diplomatic maneuver.

Globalization encouraged by America's sense of mission reached a turning point, however, with the Vietnam War. To furnish sufficient manpower for conducting the war in Southeast Asia, the Selective Service had to increase significantly the drafting, or conscription, of civilians. This step, the involuntary induction of citizens into the armed forces, accounted for much of the protests and general unpopularity of the war. The lack of a clear statement of the war's aims and the inability by the federal government to demonstrate how the Vietnamese Communists posed a threat to the United States also eroded much of the original support for the conflict.

Because of its highly controversial nature and outcome—ultimate defeat—the Vietnam War caused the United States to take a more restrained attitude toward intervention and show less willingness to commit its resources, particularly manpower, to its anti-Communist crusade. The experience in Vietnam produced a sense of demoralization because many believed the United States had backed an illegitimate government and that the use of U.S. resources for the war was "immoral and corrupting." Senator J. William Fulbright, an original supporter of the intervention in Vietnam, concluded that American action there amounted to an "arrogance of power."[10] The distasteful and bitter experience resulted in a feeling of skepticism among a large segment of the population toward overseas ventures, so that until the Cold War ended in 1989, the United States used more restraint in foreign affairs. Succeeding presidents would resort to subterfuge and covert operations in their struggle against communism.

For the growth and spread of globalization insofar as the United States was concerned, the bitter war in Southeast Asia had great importance. It brought a reassessment of the notion that America, whether for moral or economic reasons, should react to uprisings inspired by Marxists or other anti-American forces. Regardless of the reasons for its origins, the Cold War was the catalyst for American globalization, driving the country relentlessly around the globe to supplant unfriendly or threatening political movements. While factors other than the Cold War accounted for the U.S. role in the establishment of an integrated world economy, the determination to fight tyranny and take a leadership position for the sake of democracy and human rights—described as the sense of mission—suffered a serious injury with the Vietnam War. The campaign against communism did not stop with the war, but the rush to resort to intervention diminished.

The globalization of the arms race induced by the Cold War continued after the Vietnam debacle. In order to check the power and influence of Marxist or pro-Soviet regimes, the United States sold military hardware to friendly nations in various regions of the world. Corporations in the defense industry grew until critics warned about a "military-industrial complex" and excessive armament stockpiling. Both superpowers became arms suppliers to the world, but each took care not to let its weapons, and particularly its technology, slip into enemy hands. America's allies, especially Europeans, likewise engaged in the sale of arms. Fighter planes were popular, for example, among countries of the Middle East, which supplied oil to the United States and Europe. Arms sales helped Western industrial nations balance their deficit payments caused by importing oil. Civilians employed by the defense industries, apart from military personnel stationed at military bases, lived overseas to maintain the aircraft. This global race raised the armaments level overall and thrust an unprecedented amount of weapons into Third World countries of nearly all political persuasions. Marxist governments and fascist-style dictators benefited from the arms race and often reinforced their aggression with sophisticated arms and equipment. When the Cold War ended, the world was armed to the teeth. Even if the United States did not need to worry any longer about Soviet aggression, it still had to contend with small-country dictators in possession of modern arsenals. Just as economics and technology were globalized, so, too, were arms.

The iron grip of the Soviet Union in Eastern Europe began to crumble in the 1980s, marked by the fall of the Berlin Wall in 1989. Russia's own internal rifts deepened until 1992, when the Union of Soviet Socialist Republics (USSR) ceased to exist. Ethnic and national identities accounted for a large part of the dissatisfaction with Soviet rule, but the underlying cause for the fall of communism in Europe was the inability of the rulers to provide a reasonable standard of living for their citizens. Russia's well-known lag in housing, its shortages of food, and its severe lack of consumer goods created a deeply rooted dissatisfaction that ultimately drove Russia's own people, as well as those in Soviet satellite countries, into rebellion.

Globalization was a factor in this epic event, although its linkage may be difficult to see. In the 1970s the Soviet Union began to experience economic difficulties. It had to import grain because its agricultural production was insufficient to supply its domestic needs. New global corporations, or transnationals, were kept out of the Soviet sphere. The birth rate fell, and the USSR had the highest infant mortality rate among the industrialized nations. Television, a principal instrument of information technology, began to have an impact when sets became common in Soviet households in the 1980s. Western news coverage overpowered the staid official news of the Communist government. Indeed, "the Soviet Union, whether the Party liked it or not, had been drawn into a global media structure, in which the West was setting the agenda."[11]

By the 1980s the West had also begun to implement much of the cutting-edge technology connected with the Information Age.[12] Partly because of the new communication satellites and the surge in information technology, economic improvement generally occurred in the open-market countries, and although serious flaws and disparities in income remained, the standard of living rose. By its own ideological and economic rigidity, Russia fell further behind despite the efforts at reform by Premier Mikhail Gorbachev. In 1991, Boris Yeltsin seized power from Gorbachev, which is considered the collapse of the government. Russia's persistent inability to provide for its citizens and their growing awareness of the world outside their country—a process induced by globalized information—received the most credit for explaining the fall.

By contrast, America's consumer-goods market grew throughout the Cold War. A set of circumstances was responsible: the pent-up demand from the Great Depression and World War II, the baby boom, and the Cold War itself that spurred government spending for military purposes. In Europe and Japan a similar phenomenon occurred, helped in great part by American foreign aid and recovery programs such as the Marshall Plan, as noted earlier. In the United States military spending in the name of the anti-Communist crusade kept employment and consumer confidence high. The result was a growing economy based on housing, consumer goods, and the amenities of life for a half-century that furnished investment funds for research. These Cold War–induced stimuli were behind much of the new technologies associated with globalization by the end of the century.

The collapse of the Soviet Union left the United States as the sole superpower. As the military, economic, and technological giant, it stood as the winner in the fifty-year struggle between capitalism and socialism. Analysts attributed the reasons for America's triumph to its globalized economy and saw the military and security component of the Cold War as just one facet of the superpower struggle. "In the long sweep of time," wrote one scholar, "America's half-century-long ideological, political, and military face-off with the Soviet Union may appear far less consequential than America's leadership in inaugurating an era of global economic interdependence."[13]

Globalization involved more than the military and diplomatic activities undertaken by the United States in the name of the Cold War. Trade ranked alongside the struggle against communism as a force that was moving the world toward an integrated economy. Trade initiatives, in fact, preceded the Truman Doctrine and Marshall Plan, even if the Cold War involved the United States in world affairs on a level never seen before. Over the years, however, the struggle against communism forced millions of military and civilian personnel into duty around the world; it led to the creation of foreign aid programs and various security alliances; it forced the United States to exert influence at many troublesome hot spots, including two wars; and it kept a large portion of the economy involved in and dependent upon foreign sales, ranging from defense corporations building fighter planes to farmers raising wheat. It made the United States the Free World leader, the force of Pax Americana.

The vision of a new world order in 1945 presented the country with an opportunity to mold circumstances as best as possible according to the principles set forth in the Atlantic Charter: "liberty of expression, of religion, and the right to live protected from need and from fear." When the Cold War injected itself into history, the United States, motivated by a sense of mission, created a global approach to fight for its economic livelihood and its own security. No longer could the country remain aloof and depend passively on the flow of events to sustain it in the new world of nationalistic and economic realignments. Only by endeavoring with its allies for action and reaction could it expect to achieve and maintain a secure place in the world's power structure. Through each diplomatic and military adventure, whether successful or justified, the United States extended itself into regions around the world, acting as a global power and aligning the opponents of communism into an interconnected merger of common interests.

NOTES

1. Walter A. McDougal, *Promised Land, Crusader State: The American Encounter with the World since 1776* (Boston: Houghton Mifflin, 1997), 173.
2. Robert A. Divine, *Second Chance: The Triumph of Internationalism in America during World War II* (New York: Atheneum, 1967), 47–74.
3. Original quote appears in ibid., 248.
4. Original quote appears in ibid., 287.
5. Quote appears in Stephen Ambrose, *Rise to Globalism: American Foreign Policy since 1938*, 6th rev. ed. (New York: Penguin Books, 1991), 85.
6. Pells, *Not Like Us*, 54.
7. Ambrose, *Rise to Globalism*, 85.
8. Ronald Steel, *Pax Americana* (New York: Viking Press, 1967), 41.
9. Diane B. Kunz, *Butter and Guns: America's Cold War Economic Diplomacy* (New York: Free Press, 1997), 94.
10. Steven W. Hook and John Spanier, *American Foreign Policy since World War II*, 15th ed. (Washington, DC: CQ Press, 2000), 147.
11. Paul Dukes, *The Superpowers: A Short History* (London: Routledge, 2000), 141.
12. Murray Laver, *Information Technology: Agent of Change* (Cambridge, Eng.: Cambridge University Press, 1989), 28–29.
13. David M. Kennedy, *Freedom from Fear: The American People in Depression and War, 1929–1945* (New York: Oxford University Press, 1999), 855.

2 | Trade and the Promotion of Globalization

Since 1945 the United States has enjoyed a strong economy with a steady rise in the standard of living. Many of the traditional goals of families and consumers have become commonplace, to the extent that Americans expect to own their homes and automobiles, send their children to college, have access to health care, and purchase consumer goods on a regular basis. There were and continue to be inconsistencies in income and living standards, but the overall thrust of the economy has been toward prosperity. This state of affairs is due to several reasons, but the country's leadership and participation in establishing a globally integrated economy was a major factor.

In 1945, however, the United States believed it faced an impending crisis: a return to the dark days of the Great Depression. The Cold War had not become fully apparent, and the country wanted to demobilize and bring the troops home as quickly as possible. Thousands of World War II veterans would need jobs. In 1944, Congress had begun authorizing public works projects in order to pump federal dollars into the economy once military spending stopped. Congress passed the Employment Act of 1946, declaring that the government had a responsibility for maintaining conditions favorable for full employment. This sense of urgency for action to avoid another depression received reinforcement from the belief that the country's trade policies and practices prior to the war had been harmful.

After World War I the United States and other Western industrialized nations had practiced economic "protectionism," meaning that instead of encouraging trade and the free flow of goods and services, they had resorted to closing their doors to their trading partners by erecting tariff walls and other forms of protection. Protectionism had become popular after the Great War, owing to the suspicion and mistrust bred by the war and to the rise of industrial interests who exerted influence in government capitals in order to protect themselves from competitors. Protectionism now fell into disfavor. Americans regarded it as a cause of World War II, thinking that if the industrial nations of the West had practiced free trade or had at least maintained a more open trading environment, the economic woes of Germany and other European nations might have been avoided. Prosperous economies in Europe, so the reasoning went, would have encouraged democracy and likely prevented the rise of fascism. The victorious Allies in 1919 had foolishly required enormous reparations from Germany, and the American practice of making large loans to Germany only postponed the fall of its economy and the Weimar Republic, which came in 1933.

The United States' own practices had weakened the world economy during the interwar years. To begin with, it did not alter its trade and lending practices to accommodate its status as a creditor nation, a new condition wrought by World War I. Its substantial loans to other countries propped up unsound and unstable elements of their economies. Poor lending practices by American investors, caught in the speculative frenzy of the 1920s, falsely maintained weak overseas companies. The recipients of these loans, located mostly in Europe, Canada, and Latin America, were unable to sell their products in the U.S. market because of the tariff barrier. The Fordney-McCumber Tariff of 1922 restored the protective wall of the late nineteenth century, and the Hawley-Smoot Tariff of 1930, coming at the onset of the Great Depression, was one of the highest tariffs in U.S. history. Unable to sell in the American market, the other countries could not accumulate the funds needed to pay back the loans, making for an unsound and unstable world economy. "This policy, so typical of the 1920s," wrote one economic historian, "was too fantastic to last even if world economic relations had been on a sound and stable basis."[1] When the depression hit, the loans stopped and the economies dependent on them went flat.

During the 1930s international commerce became even more constrained. Two of the principal trading partners of the United States, Germany and Japan, restricted their trade in order to become self-sufficient, and producers of both industrial and agricultural goods lost significant markets. Britain established its "Imperial System" in 1932 with the Ottawa Conference, which granted preferential trading rights to members of the Commonwealth. France took a similar step with its closed-market system. A clumsy network of import quotas, licensing, and currency exchanges added to the restrictive nature of international trade. The United States sought encouragement with the Reciprocal Trade Act of 1934, but the measure brought little improvement. Any trade agreements made by countries tended to be unilateral, and there was no general sense of cooperation or willingness to reform the structure of international trade.

Viewing history from the perspective of 1945, American political and business interests generally agreed that protectionism and isolationism had proved to be the twin sisters of economic and military disaster. The Great Depression and two world wars seemed to prove the foolishness of hiding behind walls and moats, and a new attitude and mentality—based on engaging the United States and other countries, East and West, in international trade—had to be followed if history were not to repeat itself. Trade, even before the Cold War, earned new respect and was regarded as the key to restoring the economies of both the United States and at least its traditional trading partners. Working with the advantage of hindsight plus the sense of urgency not to let the economy slide back into depression, the United States wanted to reverse the world's trade practices of the past generation and jump eagerly into the postwar era intent upon rebuilding the global economy as well as its own. The nation's historic sense of mission sat atop this conviction, so that for the rest of the century, free trade was a common ideology of both Republicans and Democrats, and succeeding presidents pursued such a course irrespective of their other differences. "For leaders in Washington," observed two scholars of international studies, "recent history showed that American prosperity and security depended upon an economically stable and open world order."[2]

Proponents of free trade, or freer trade, followed the fundamental economic principle known as comparative advantage, set forth by David Ricardo in 1817. It meant that each country produces some goods and commodities at a greater level of efficiency and at a lower cost than other countries—it has a comparative advantage on those particular items. It behooves each country to maximize its production of those items and export them as much as possible. The same country should, however, import those goods and commodities for which it has a comparative disadvantage. Through this process, trading partners can achieve their highest level of efficiency and enhance their level of prosperity. Comparative advantage was a key ingredient in the rationale for globalization and received much attention in the last half-century.

Toward the end of World War II the United States realized that for the West European nations to restore their economies, upon which the future of the U.S. economy depended, a new financial order that would place international currencies on a stable basis had to be erected. The chaos of the depression and the devastation wrought by the war had greatly weakened the financial foundations of Europe and Asia, so plans got under way in 1943 to institute a new international financial system, which resulted in the Bretton Woods Conference of 1944.

As an example of American leadership in globalization, the establishment of the International Monetary Fund (IMF) and the World Bank at the conference stands out. Motivated by the compelling need to reconstruct the world's economy in the aftermath of death and destruction, economists and policy analysts from forty-four countries met in New Hampshire to design a plan for restoring financial integrity to war-torn countries and for rebuilding the infrastructure of trade. Because of their system of imperial preference, the British had conducted trade with pounds sterling prior to the war, and the French through their system of closed markets had done the same with francs. Because of the natural barrier imposed by these systems, but especially because of the weaknesses of these currencies and others caused by the war, there was a natural inclination to erect a more stable monetary system, an essential factor for restoring trade and prosperity. To Bretton Woods from Britain came the famous economist John Maynard Keynes, and heading the American delegation was Harry Dexter White. This meeting proved to be an intriguing episode in modern history with ramifications for the growth of an integrated world economy.

Keynes was a brilliant economist and strategist, but White managed to get a mostly American plan approved because of the dominating economic and military position of the United States. Both men agreed not to return to the classic gold standard that had been used until the 1930s depression, but fixed the U.S. dollar to gold, which would be convertible at $35 per ounce, and persuaded other countries to fix their currencies to the dollar. If a country's currency weakened, it could borrow from the IMF to bolster its economy and thereby the soundness of its currency. The plan was to establish a stable system of currency exchange rates and to help nations overcome occasional trouble in maintaining their foreign payments requirements. Funds for the loans came from IMF member nations. Cooperation among them was the goal in order to achieve and maintain monetary stability, but it also intended to bring poorer countries into the world economy.

As a second and complementary part to this system of currency exchange, the conferees created the International Bank for Reconstruction and Development, known as the World Bank. Again, member nations provided capital, with the United States accounting for about one-third of the total and Britain supplying about 15 percent. The Bank was empowered to make loans to countries for infrastructure projects: roads, dams, factories, schools, railroads, and the like. After the mid-1950s, the World Bank concentrated mostly, but not entirely, on developing countries. In both cases, the institutions could impose conditions for the loans.

Such a system of linkage was intended to provide stable exchange rates for commercial transactions between countries. The value of each nation's currency depended on its balance of trade, and if its balance fell too low, a country could request an adjustment in its currency rate. In other words, the fixed exchange rate established at Bretton Woods represented an attempt to stabilize world currencies and encourage trade. The United States in particular sought the last point, an improved environment for free trade, which it reasoned would benefit its own economy and also overcome the awkward structure of international trade in practice on the eve of World War II. "The presumption was," as was stated in one case, "that a free-trading, nondiscriminatory environment would offer the benefits of peaceful economic competition, equal access to raw materials, and maximum efficiency through the principle of comparative advantage."[3]

Successful and steady growth occurred among the Western trading partners in the fifteen-year period after the war, but the system established at Bretton Woods was only part of the American effort to rebuild the world economy. Foreign aid as seen in the Marshall Plan or the U.S. reconstruction efforts in occupied Japan overshadowed the impact of the IMF or the World Bank, but the latter was nonetheless important.

Another arm of American economic policy with global implications was the Export-Import Bank. Created in the 1930s to provide credit to foreign nations wishing to buy U.S. products, the Bank extended loans to America's allies during World War II. It continued funding badly needed reconstruction projects after the war. Foreign private interests, such as textile mills in Germany and Japan, for example, also received loans for industrial development. The Bank operated in the context of American international objectives, so its loans went for projects that would rebuild and enhance world trade. A spirit of humanitarianism was behind the loans, too, so it must not be assumed that the various forms of economic assistance rested solely on selfish interests. The effect of the Export-Import Bank in promoting an integrated world economy was more subtle than the IMF or the World Bank, but it nonetheless served as an instrument of U.S. economic policy. As would be expected, the United States used the Bank as an economic weapon in the Cold War, granting loans to friendly nations and coercing or rewarding its allies for their support and cooperation in foreign affairs. During the Suez Crisis of 1956, the United States dangled funds from the IMF and the Export-Import Bank to obtain British withdrawal from Egypt.[4]

Looking at the development of trade after World War II from the vantage point of the twenty-first century might create the impression that little or no disagreement existed in the United States over the programs for loans or trade agreements. Free trade in its purest sense did not exist, however, because the political climate would not allow it. There remained a strong liking for protectionism at home and abroad, thus forcing the proponents of trade to exercise patience and political maneuvering. As was stated in one case, "two steps forward, one step back . . . characterized the progress of the American crusade for freer trade."[5] Protectionism never disappeared, but it had its greatest influence for the first fifteen to twenty years after the war.

Special interests preferred the protection from foreign competition afforded by high tariffs. They exerted pressure on Congress, particularly the Republican Party, which contained most of the remnants of isolationism. The New Deal's program for stimulating international commerce, based on the Reciprocal Trade Act of 1934, continued into the 1940s, but only bilateral agreements could be made, or a simple exchange program between the United States and one country. The much broader practice of multilateralism did not start gaining wide popularity until the latter 1960s and 1970s. Indeed, the first years of the postwar era witnessed stiff resistance to a liberal trade order. Bilateral agreements generally had to include escape clauses at the requests of special interests in order to win approval. Still, the United States moved in the direction of free trade.

Roosevelt's secretary of state, Cordell Hull, had been the champion of free trade among Washington officialdom since his appointment in 1933. He urged the creation of an international trade organization (ITO) in order to facilitate agreements and set forth his concept in 1945 with an official document, "Proposals for Expansion of World Trade and Employment." Hull thought a set of rules agreed upon by members of an ITO could promptly resolve trade issues and expedite the flow of goods and services. Based on Hull's proposals, a conference representing twenty-three countries, mostly from the West, met in Geneva, Switzerland, in 1947. By coming together as a group, the representatives quickly set down rules and negotiated an agreement reducing trade barriers, known as the General Agreement on Tariffs and Trade (GATT). Indicative of the differing opinions in the United States over the concept of free trade was Congress's refusal to ratify GATT or U.S. membership in the proposed ITO. GATT nonetheless went into operation because of President Truman's use of authority based on the Reciprocal Trade Act, but Hull's proposed ITO required congressional approval and it never passed.

GATT represented the new spirit of cooperation extant in the Western world after World War II and was a contrast with the earlier mentality of protectionism. It did not establish free trade, but through a series of meetings staggered over one half-century it managed to reduce the barriers to trade and thereby served as a principal instrument of globalization. Until it became the World Trade Organization (WTO) in 1994, GATT held seven meetings generally known as "Rounds." Tariff reduction occupied the attention of GATT into the 1960s, but after the Geneva meeting in 1947, when tariffs were lowered about 21 percent, progress was slower. Until the Kennedy Round of 1963–1967, reductions never exceeded a 4 percent average.

Member nations retained the right to invoke the use of escape clauses in order to protect special interests at home, and GATT recognized the right of governments to subsidize segments of their economies. GATT also exempted agriculture from its jurisdiction. A critical element of GATT, taken from the Reciprocal Trade Act of 1934, was the principle of "most favored nation," which required each nation to grant the same tariff duty it arranged with another country to all GATT members. This principle struck down discrimination among trading partners, which had been a common practice in the prewar years. In the words of one noted economist, "This allows comparative advantage to be the main determinant of trade patterns, which promotes global efficiency."[6]

GATT brought a new advantage: it served as a court of judgment to settle disputes. Member nations could take complaints or grievances before GATT for reconciliation. The organization had no authority to enforce its recommendations, however, and unless the offending nation agreed to comply with GATT's rulings, the practice could continue. It was this weakness that led partially to the creation of the WTO. Nevertheless, membership in GATT grew because nations saw the advantages of being part of a large trading bloc that included the United States and the major industrial powers of Europe.

During the first quarter-century of GATT's operations, the United States wielded considerable influence. Its power related to the world economic situation: the United States had the only powerful economy and currency at the end of World War II. It provided the single greatest market for other countries, which desperately needed to export goods and commodities in order to rebuild their economies. A common expression stated the case: "When the United States sneezes, the world catches cold." Timing was also a factor because GATT's beginning coincided with the start of the Cold War. In 1947 the Truman Doctrine was promulgated to prevent the spread of communism, and the Marshall Plan, which had strong anti-Communist implications, went into operation. Western Europe in particular relied on U.S. military and economic backing and opened its arms to America, with its design for a liberal trade order. President Eisenhower embraced the free-trade goals set forth earlier by Truman so that "by 1960," according to one account, "the American economy had become far more integrated into the world economy than wartime planners had ever anticipated."[7]

Asia had a place in the American scheme of world trade, but it was not thought to be as important as Europe because markets there had been smaller prior to the war. Japan had been the chief Asian market of the United States, whose interests now wanted to restore the trade as soon as possible. Japan received loans from the Export-Import Bank and went through a reconstruction of its industry while General Douglas MacArthur oversaw the American occupation of Japan, which ended in 1952. The Truman administration, however, gave precedence to Europe, so the amount of aid and loans to Asian countries in the earlier years were comparatively small. With the triumph of the Communists in China in 1949, however, Japan and

Southeast Asia suddenly became strategically important to the United States. An economically strong Japan, it was thought, would counter the influence of China and the Soviet Union in the Far East. Japan became a member of GATT in 1955 and proceeded to take advantage of the stable international currency system established at Bretton Woods in 1944 and the open-market environment encouraged by the United States.

An international trade boom began in the 1950s, which benefited Japan and lasted for nearly twenty years. It was due in great part to the stable international currency system carried out by the IMF and the efforts by GATT to promote commerce. According to one account, "the total volume of manufactured goods exported around the globe increased by six times, and the dollar value of world exports by more than seven." Indeed, "everyone seemed eager to trade."[8]

An important feature in understanding globalization was the place of the Communist nations in world trade. The two principal areas of Communist strength were the Soviet Union and China. In 1945 the Soviet Union refused to ratify the Bretton Woods accords and indicated to the Truman administration that it would not repay its Lend-Lease debts from World War II. It also refused to participate in the recovery program of the Marshall Plan and forced its satellites in Eastern Europe to do the same. The United States had anticipated the Soviet reaction.

Feeling the need to combat American influence in Europe, the Soviet Union established the Council of Mutual Economic Assistance (COMECON) in 1949. It was the Soviet counterpart to the Marshall Plan, but it had little substance. Through COMECON the Soviet Union made bilateral trade agreements with its satellites in Eastern Europe, but instead of aiding these smaller countries, the agreements allowed the Soviets to take commodities and products for their own benefit. Small workshops and industries were nationalized, and independent entrepreneurs and unions were crushed. Prices were often fixed and production quotas set. In all of these state-controlled satellite economies the result was low public morale, inefficiency, and underperforming industries. By the same token the United States would not make loans to them. In effect, the economic steps taken by the superpowers paralleled their security measures. China was likewise outside the Western trading sphere, and the United States refused to extend diplomatic recognition to Mao Zedong's government. By 1949 the world reached its bipolar split.

American trade with the two Communist giants had been negligible prior to World War II, and the loss of their markets meant little harm. To be sure, business interests hungrily salivated over those markets, but in 2002 they remained largely untapped. Russia and China were not, however, isolated: they traded with U.S. allies and many Third World or neutral countries and in some instances purchased commodities in the United States. In 1972 the Soviets bought $750 million worth of wheat from American granaries. From the standpoint of the United States, however, trade with the Communists remained a small portion of its international commerce and transactions.

The Communist nations remained dogmatic and restrictive, an approach that economists describe as autarkic, but Western Europe took a different approach. Washington's drumbeat for opening world markets brought about a desired result with the creation of the European Union. For the first decade after the war, 1945–1955, while the United States pushed strongly for tariff reductions, West European nations continued to rely on tariffs and various restrictions to regulate their trade. Negotiations conducted through GATT brought some reductions, however, and encouraged Europeans to think about erecting a regional trade bloc. In 1957 six nations signed the Treaty of Rome that set up the Common Market: West Germany, the Netherlands, Luxembourg, Italy, France, and Belgium. It later took in more members and became the European Union.

The Common Market began to establish a free-trade zone in which restrictions on manufactured goods would be eliminated. Along with the removal of tariffs and quotas, the major provisions included a uniform tariff on goods imported from nonmember nations, a standard agricultural policy, and an agreement to centralize monetary and fiscal policies. For the proponents of free trade, the most important element was the spirit of cooperation among the members and their willingness to construct their economies on the principle of a liberal trade system. Trade of industrial goods among the six nations jumped faster than the general rate of world trade. The success of this concept became evident as the United Kingdom, Ireland, and Denmark joined in 1973.[9]

Within the newly created Common Market were the seeds of competition for the United States. International economic leaders now paid more attention to Europe and were curious whether the Common Market would grow and become a new competitor in the world marketplace. The Common Market encouraged the rise of larger corporate firms better able to streamline production and attain greater efficiency, which would mean greater mass production and competitive prices. Such firms could also afford research and improved transportation. Some of these advantages had already been achieved through the European Coal and Steel Community (ECSC). As European companies overcame their disjointed nature, they could be expected to show a new sense of cooperation and coordination. In other words, the creation of the Common Market, if it succeeded and expanded, might cause the United States to lose its position of dominance in the world economy.[10]

For the American proponents of free trade, however, these predictions brought no fear. They saw economic growth in Europe as beneficial for them and firmly believed that a prosperous Europe stood in the path of Soviet expansion. The Common Market was the fruit borne on the branches of American aid and the Marshall Plan. For U.S. policymakers the new European alliance, by modernizing and strengthening the Continent's economy, would enhance the Bretton Woods system of fixed exchange rates and enable Europe to bear some of the burden of the struggle against communism.

Globalization of the world economy took a new turn in the early 1970s, when the United States ended the Bretton Woods system. American leadership in the postwar international economy stood on two pillars: trade and its support of the international fixed rate of exchange. For one quarter-century the United States had taken the dominant role in the management of the world economy by fostering prosperity, encouraging political stability, and acting as the global hegemon with its Pax Americana. Toward the end of the 1960s, however, Uncle Sam was in trouble. While the United States was not yet facing a crisis, it needed to adjust its position vis-à-vis international monetary exchange. This change came at the instigation of President Richard Nixon and his New Economic Policy (NEP), which came to be known as the "Nixon shocks."

Behind the "shocks" lay the new position of the United States in world trade; it had started running a deficit with its balance of payments. The amount of dollars held by other governments and foreign investors had also grown to a high level, to the point that U.S. gold reserves were not sufficient to allow convertibility of all dollars held overseas. It was not likely that holders of these dollars would demand payment in gold, although some demand could be expected. More immediate was an anticipated fall in the value of the dollar because it was so extended around the world. If confidence fell, then the United States could expect a run on the dollar. When faced with such a predicament, countries nearly always devalued their currencies. Some governments enjoying a surplus balance of payments had already devalued their currencies, but the United States had not done so because it honored the convertibility of the dollar into gold by virtue of the Bretton Woods accords. Until the late 1960s the strength of the American economy kept the 1944 arrangement acceptable, but the rising power of the Japanese and European economies made it outdated. Goods produced in the United States were less attractive abroad because of the dollar being overvalued, causing trade to suffer and employment to drop. Nixon decided to end the Bretton Woods system because, as stated by one writer, it had become "inherently biased against the American economy."[11]

Deeply rooted behind this weakened condition of the dollar were further developments. America's imports had begun exceeding exports, owing to the rising popularity of overseas goods, particularly automobiles and electronic items. America's European trading partners had started capturing some markets in COMECON countries as the Soviet Union relaxed its stranglehold on Eastern Europe, thereby costing the United States some trade with its allies on the Continent. America's growing use of foreign oil, though small by later comparisons, also eroded its favorable balance of trade. Very critical in this state of affairs was the U.S. role in the Cold War. At great cost it ensured security for Europe and Japan, which persistently furnished only a small portion of their own defense but had now become competitors in trade. Because of these new circumstances, the U.S. economy by 1970 was losing to competition while carrying a heavy Cold War burden.

In order to reverse the flow of dollars out of the country and stimulate exports, Nixon placed a 15 percent charge on all imports and stopped the conversion of dollars into gold. He also cut federal spending and set wage and price controls. As a consequence, currencies around the world, including the dollar, "floated" on the international market—that is, they fell or rose to a level of value based on the strength of the nations' economies. In the United States, economic growth returned and employment improved. Europe and Japan were displeased, but they accepted the new order because they relied on Washington for military security.

By ending the Bretton Woods arrangement, Nixon altered the world monetary system. Currencies were no longer pegged to the dollar but floated on their own merit. Gone were the safety and predictability of the Bretton Woods rules, which had been a useful as well as critical stabilizer during the postwar era. Capital now moved more easily across borders, which made available more cash for international investments and allowed the process of globalization to gain more speed.

For the rest of the century, the United States faced more complex and competitive circumstances in world trade. By the same token, the rise of competitors and their commercial intercourse advanced globalization. Markets grew around the world, and barriers, whether political or economic, fell and opened new opportunities for trade. Consumers in the developed countries enjoyed a wide range of imported products, but they became dependent upon one another for their rising standard of living. Facing stiff competition, the United States stuck nonetheless with its belief that free trade offered the best opportunity to strengthen the economies of developed countries and advance those in the developing world. The new competition, particularly from Japan, revived sentiment for protection in the United States and brought sporadic restrictions on imports, but the general thrust of trade policy remained based on the principle of free access to markets.

In the post–Bretton Woods era, the United States faced an increasing and exasperating dependence on foreign oil, considered by environmentalists to be the result of gluttony and by others to be the consequence of a rising standard of living. Apart from analyses and explanations, Americans simply used more oil, and therein lay a significant factor in the globalization of the United States. By 2000 nearly 50 percent of U.S. oil supplies came from foreign sources, primarily Saudi Arabia, Kuwait, and Iran in the Middle East, and Mexico and Venezuela in Latin America. A new word appeared in the vocabulary of trade, "petrodollars," which referred to dollars spent on foreign oil and then transversed through the global economy. A significant share of the petrodollars came to rest in American banks. These petrodollars in effect added to the world's stock of capital and served to finance a wide variety of projects around the globe. The large amount of dollars in circulation, plus the ability of the United States to maintain a sound currency, went a long way in keeping the dollar as the dominant currency in the world, even after President Nixon ended the convertibility of the dollar in 1971.

During the 1970s the United States suffered from "stagflation" as its deficit balance of payments continued to grow. In several areas of the economy, Japanese and European manufacturers further expanded their share of the U.S. domestic market. American steel industry leaders, for example, overlooked the new forces of global competition and fell victim to the more efficiently produced and lower-cost steel from overseas, so that by the mid-1970s many of the major mills in the United States, a source of American industrial pride, shut down. Across the industrial heartland the term "Rust Belt" came into use, referring to the deteriorated condition of steel and other heavy industries. A similar process, though not as disastrous, hit the automobile industry when drivers turned to smaller and more fuel-efficient Japanese Hondas, Toyotas, and other foreign makes of cars. Manufacturers moved into other countries to escape rising labor costs and growing environmental regulations, as well as to position themselves geographically for better global distribution of their products.

All of these developments began earnestly in the 1970s and could be attributed to highly competitive corporations in various countries able to penetrate overseas markets. While the American market experienced newcomers from other lands, U.S. corporations were just as successful in establishing a presence overseas. Probably the best-known example is McDonald's, which opened its famous Golden Arches hamburger outlets in major cities around the globe, including Tokyo in 1971 and Moscow in 1990. (See Chapter 6.)

By the 1980s the momentum of the world, or at least the leading industrial nations, toward an integrated economy sped forward. Large corporations realized the potential for greater profit and security by extending their operations beyond the borders of their home country. New sources of capital were available, including petrodollars, and by taking advantage of new technologies and improved infrastructure in previously undeveloped areas, internationally oriented corporations, commonly known as transnationals, began to emerge. These new giants were among the first to see the advantages of operating on a global scale. Japanese, European, and American firms fought a capitalistic war, penetrating world markets and stealing customers from each other.

At the same time, GATT's member nations often resorted to various tactics to protect special interests; bilateral agreements and subsidies of industries were popular methods of erecting walls. This inconsistent behavior of lowering tariffs and raising other barriers came from the needs of particular industries. In fact, when industries lose their competitive edge, they will then exert their influence for government protection from overseas manufacturers. Hence, a GATT nation may have agreed to a lower tariff rate but will find new devices to block imports. For this reason, trade negotiations, including the resolution of disputes, are conducted on an ongoing basis. By the 1980s, GATT appeared to be weakening, and it needed to address two new areas of trade: services and intellectual property. There was a growing conviction, too, that it should confront the agricultural trade that had generally been omitted from GATT negotiations.

Certainly the most successful GATT negotiations occurred with the Uruguay Round conducted from 1986 to 1993. It achieved much success in removing nontariff barriers and established the most uniform set of rules up to that point. Tariffs fell a remarkable average of 40 percent, and some items such as steel and pharmaceuticals were freed from import duties. Some countries opened their doors to the new area of financial services. Better protection for copyrights, highly sought by drug companies, also came out of the Uruguay Round. Only minimal progress, however, was made in reducing barriers to agricultural trade, which had always been a sensitive area. A milestone occurred during the Round when negotiators agreed to recommend the creation of a new international trade organization, the dream of Cordell Hull, which became the World Trade Organization in 1994. Much of the impetus for the WTO rose from the concern over the growing power of three large sectors: Europe, the Americas, and a portion of Asia. The proponents of the WTO wished to avoid segmenting international trade along the lines of these sectors and hoped that a single organization would maintain a free-trade environment.

During the 1990s there existed a new public awareness over the importance of trade. The dissolution of the Soviet Union and the fall of communism in Eastern Europe reminded the world of the strength of capitalism and its emphasis on spontaneous freedom. The rigid and dogmatic economic plans of Europe's socialist countries disappeared, and in their place came the hope to build free- and open-market societies. Opportunities for economic growth also appeared in Latin America and portions of Asia.

These political developments coincided with new technologies that fostered international trade, and a wave of energy and enthusiasm swept the globe. Venture capitalists eagerly anticipated entering the former socialist countries just as people there eagerly awaited consumer goods from the West. Regional trade blocs gained popularity owing in part to their increasing power as well as to the recognition by countries of the value in belonging to a bloc with a common trade interest. In 1991 the Common Market became the European Union, with a much-expanded membership. Since World War II free trade had never received such support. In 1998 the Brookings Institution wrote that "the performance of the U.S. economy since 1992 has been the best in a generation."[12] The genie was out of the bottle. Globalization accelerated.

Trade blocs had existed for a generation, but only the European Union had great power. Various countries now rushed to position themselves to take advantage of the opportunities afforded by globalization. The Asia Pacific Economic Cooperation, founded in 1989, focused on trade in the Pacific Basin. The Mercado Comun del Cono Sur (MERCOSUR), established in 1991 by Argentina, Brazil, Paraguay, and Uruguay, became the major bloc of Latin America. In 1994 the Common Market for Eastern and Southern Africa commenced operations. For North America, the North American Free Trade Agreement (NAFTA) went into operation in 1994.

NAFTA, an agreement among the United States, Canada, and Mexico, is the world's second-largest trade bloc. The United States ratified and joined NAFTA only after a long and arduous debate that carried over into the presidential campaign of 1992. Like any trade agreement, NAFTA sought to reduce tariffs and other barriers for the sake of business growth and prosperity. In the past the United States maintained restrictions on Mexican imports, but NAFTA removed or greatly reduced them.

This new agreement aroused considerable controversy. Little opposition erupted over the 1988 agreement between the United States and Canada, but when it was proposed to add Mexico, opposition quickly appeared. Ross Perot, the third-party candidate for president in 1992, predicted that the American economy would suffer substantially if NAFTA became operational. During the congressional debates over ratification, labor and environmental interests expressed fear over damage to the environment and loss of jobs, particularly to assembly plants, known as *maquiladoras*, expected to open along the border. There was also some concern over food safety since the United States imported foodstuffs from Mexico where pollution controls were comparatively less stringent. Only after changes were made to accommodate the objections from labor and environmentalists did Congress ratify the agreement.

Defenders and critics of NAFTA maintained websites on the Internet where they published data and their rationale for supporting or attacking the agreement. Like most topics on globalization, an objective analysis of NAFTA was rare, but the North American Integration and Development Center at the University of California at Los Angeles presented evidence in January 2000 that U.S.-Mexican trade had begun to grow about ten years prior to the implementation of NAFTA. The reduced tariffs wrought by NAFTA had little impact on Mexican imports to the United States. In fact, those items not free of tariffs had the fastest growth rate, encouraging the Center to conclude that up to the time of its study, the trade between the countries had indeed grown but NAFTA's impact had been negligible. In regard to jobs, the study showed a loss of 37,000 per year in the United States, but since the American economy produced about 200,000 new jobs per year, the benefits of trade with Mexico outweighed the losses. Real suffering nonetheless occurred among those losing jobs, and the Center suggested some form of unemployment relief for them.[13]

An example of the criticism of NAFTA came from UNITE (Union of Needletrades, Industrial, and Textile Employees). According to this organization, the United States has "lost thousands of jobs because of NAFTA."[14] The U.S.-Mexican border had furthermore become a health hazard that grew worse each year, due to the relocation of American manufacturing plants there to escape U.S. pollution regulations. Prior to NAFTA the United States, so UNITE contended, had a trade surplus with Mexico but developed a deficit after the agreement went into effect because American manufacturers shipped their Mexican-assembled products into the United States. NAFTA also allegedly caused the loss of 250,000 jobs. The organization blamed Mexico's peso crisis and Chiapas uprising on NAFTA. Only transnational corporations, it claimed, benefited from the agreement. From the point of view of this union of mostly textile workers, the United States should strive for the following in Mexico: the right to unionize, health and safety standards, and prohibition of child labor.[15]

An example of the counterargument defending NAFTA came from the Heritage Foundation. It insisted that the United States had not lost thousands of jobs and its manufacturing base had not been weakened. From 1994 to 1997, the Foundation claimed, exports to Mexico increased 30 percent and U.S. employment wages rose. In a state-by-state analysis of exports to Canada and Mexico, the report claimed that only six states experienced no increases. The southern states, according to the Foundation, benefited the most from exports to Mexico.

These website battles reflect the different perceptions of globalization. Active and bona fide representatives of business, labor, and academe made conflicting claims about NAFTA and other topics generally related to the impact of open trade. Interpretation of the data and perspective taken almost certainly affected the judgment of analysts, so that a final conclusion may be impossible to reach. The peso crisis of 1995 seriously upset the Mexican economy and made NAFTA's effect almost impossible to judge, at least temporarily. Loss of jobs seemed to be a legitimate claim, particularly for textile and apparel workers, but the creation of new jobs owing to trade stood as an equally viable claim. Proponents of globalization saw a net increase in jobs, even though they usually acknowledged that workers in some industries suffered. The most common proposal for disaffected workers included unemployment relief and training in new job skills.

Other nations in the Western Hemisphere tapped the huge American apparel market. The Caribbean Basin Initiative (CBI) passed by Congress in 2000 approved the duty-free import of textiles manufactured in CBI countries from yarn spun in the United States. Two American interests in particular benefited from the CBI: cotton and wool producers and textile spinners. The ten CBI member countries included Honduras, Guatemala, and Jamaica.

Superseding the regional trade blocs, at least in its intent and purpose, was the WTO, which, as noted earlier, became operational in 1995. It was the only fully global trade organization, with 139 members. The WTO provided some advantages and greater responsibilities than GATT. While the latter's members remained bound to the GATT agreements of the past, the WTO could bring the newly sensitive issues of services, particularly intellectual property, into negotiations. Agreements made by the WTO would also be binding on all member nations, thus stopping the practice of some GATT members of not following the rules.

The WTO had the unprecedented authority to negotiate agricultural trade, which had been purposefully neglected by GATT because countries were reluctant to subject their farm interests to world competition. Developed countries such as the United States subsidized farmers, and in Japan the government protected rice growers because the Japanese sense of community and concept of collective action was rooted in rice farming. The United States and Japan had a dispute over rice because American rice producers believed they deserved access to the Japanese market, since Japan had penetrated the U.S. market in automobiles and electronics. The artificial barriers in agriculture, which had not been addressed in the past, provided another reason for the creation of the WTO. Like GATT, it could arbitrate disputes, but it also had the authority to order compensation for a nation subjected to unfair practices. Any nation refusing to comply faced retaliation. By 2002 the WTO had not resolved the dispute over the alleged exploitation of cheap labor in developing countries, however, nor had it overcome the impact of trade on the world's environment.

Partly because of these issues, the WTO was the target of demonstrations in Seattle in December 1999. Negotiators planned a summit meeting there to review unfinished business from the Uruguay Round and to address recurring issues regarding agriculture, textiles, and services. They also planned to deal with the question of damage to the environment wrought by the globalized economy.

About 50,000 protestors took to the streets; they hoped to scuttle the summit meeting. They brought attention to globalization and wanted to make the WTO appear to be an instrument of ruthless capitalism and heartless transnationals. Negotiators achieved little and the meeting failed. Negotiators had their own reasons, however, for the lack of progress, particularly their differences over labor, because developing countries resented any intrusion into their economies for the sake of reform. With no progress in Seattle, the WTO continued to arbitrate disputes and plan for another summit conference. In the meantime, differences between the United States and its major trading partners over agriculture and services persisted.

The public scrutiny placed on international trade by the Seattle outbreak made the IMF and the World Bank targets of the antiglobalists, who regarded both institutions as instruments employed by the developed nations to enrich their own economies and maintain their supremacy in the integrated world economy. They often saw trade agreements as devices that enabled special interests to exploit the resources of the Third World without any safeguards for people who may have suffered injurious effects from open trade. Despite the mission of the IMF and the World Bank to reduce poverty, critics insist that they have the opposite effect. "Most of the world's most impoverished countries have suffered under IMF/World Bank programs for two decades," stated Mobilization for Global Justice. "They've seen debt levels rise, unemployment skyrocket, poverty increase, and environments devastated."[16] Critics charge trade organizations with favoring investors and transnational corporations over the common man in order to protect massive loans or even to maintain the political and economic status quo in poor countries.

Critics also look upon the IMF as a misbegotten institution created at Bretton Woods in 1944 in order to replace or maintain old-fashioned Western imperialism with the euphemism of development. Instead of imposing a blunt and offensive control onto an undeveloped country, the rich nations of the West allegedly designed a gentler technique of open trade to ensure a supply of resources for themselves. One writer asserted: "Development is just a new word for what Marxists called *imperialism* and what we can loosely refer to as *colonialism*—a more familiar and less loaded term."[17] One strong critic of transnational corporations believed that "the two main Bretton Woods institutions, the World Bank and the International Monetary Fund, have become principal tools by which the new global managers maintain corporate control over nations and peoples."[18] Such accusations have not caused any reassessments or readjustments of policy in the world economy, but they demonstrate the frustration and anger of opponents. In April 2000, for example, demonstrators clashed with police when they protested a conference of the IMF and the World Bank in Washington, DC.[19]

The IMF seeks to encourage and maintain a stable balance of payments and strong currencies among its 183 member nations, and when it makes loans to them, usually short-term, it nearly always stipulates conditions that must be met. Generally the borrowing countries have one or a combination of the following: a balance-of-payments deficit, a large national debt, an unstable monetary policy, and excessive public spending, which usually results in a weak currency. Recipient countries may have to reduce public spending, buy fewer imports, and pay down their national debt. When these steps of austerity, along with the loan, fail to correct the imbalance of payments and set off unemployment or inflation, civil unrest often occurs. Protestors often blame the IMF for the weakened economy.

More moderate critics of the IMF regard it as a useful weapon in the fight for global prosperity, but one in need of reform. More effort should be made, for example, to soften the impact of the IMF's required loans on the working classes of the Third World. In 1998, when the IMF demanded higher interest rates in a bailout plan for Brazil to stabilize the currency, some economists believed it would be wiser to let the nation's currency float and thus find its new value via the world market, or establish a currency board to regulate the Brazilian economy. Due to criticism of its policies inaugurated in Indonesia in 1998, the IMF relaxed its restrictions, which permitted the government to slow the cost of food. In defending the organization, the IMF's Stanley Fisher stated, "It's our job to convince people to do things that we believe, and they probably know, are good for them. Even if those things are politically unpopular—and they usually are."[20]

The World Bank has a different purpose and thereby escapes some of the harsher criticism and anger. Its loans generally stretch over a longer period of time and are usually designed for physical improvements, which people in recipient countries tend to see as positive benefits. The IMF's loans focus on immediate issues, however, usually a currency crisis, and serve to avert further deterioration of the currency with fast-acting remedies. Thus, its actions often impose painful correcting mechanisms, whereas World Bank loans generate visible improvements.

After the Seattle fiasco, speculation and fear arose that protectionism had started to resurface. Skeptics of globalization proliferated. Opponents used the technology of globalization, the Internet, to organize and stage protests at conferences of the IMF and the World Bank. Critics linked globalization with genetically modified crops, known as Bt (biotechnology) food, seeing it as a danger to public health. Some global food companies responded to the pressure and restricted their use of Bt commodities. Alarming concerns over the danger of food across borders set off a demand for regulating the global market.

Despite the stigma attached to globalization, only partly due to the Seattle demonstrations, a liberal trade order still existed in the world in 2002. It began as an object of reformers who, at the end of World War II, saw international commerce as the best possible antidote to economic depression as well as to mistrust and suspicion among countries. For the past half-century the United States took the leadership role, using trade as an instrument to restore the world economy and fight communism. "We are the giant of the economic world," President Truman told an audience in 1947. "Whether we like it or not, the future pattern of economic relations depends on us."[21] The United States had to adjust via the Nixon shocks at about the midway point, which came in 1971 because its trading partners had become powerful. Prosperity is not automatic, of course, and economies rise and fall, but the world's standard of living at the end of the century was a great improvement from 1945, and trade helped make it happen. The collapse of communism in Europe reinforced the argument of the free traders. For the first time in modern American history, however, trade rules had become an object of public concern and protest, a result of the growing suspicion of globalization. Because of questions and apprehensions, the integration of the world economy may slow, but it will not stop. Forces other than trade policy push globalization forward, and perhaps the most important is technology.

NOTES

1. Harold U. Faulkner, *American Economic History*, 8th ed. (New York: Harper and Brothers, 1960), 686.
2. William H. Becker and Samuel F. Wells Jr., *Economics and World Power: An Assessment of American Diplomacy since 1789* (New York: Columbia University Press, 1984), 335.
3. Ibid.
4. Kunz, *Butter and Guns*, 86–87.
5. Ibid., 295.
6. Robert J. Carbaugh, *International Economics*, 7th ed. (Cincinnati: South-Western College Publishing, 2000), 192.
7. Ibid., 3; quote appears in Becker and Wells, *Economics and World Power*, 354.
8. Gary D. Allison, *Japan's Postwar History* (Ithaca, NY: Cornell University Press, 1997), 99.
9. Carbaugh, *International Economics*, 274–75.
10. Irving B. Kravis, "The U.S. Common Position and the Common Market," in *The Common Market: Progress and Controversy*, ed. Lawrence B. Krause (Englewood Cliffs, NJ: Prentice-Hall, 1964), 136–59.
11. Becker and Wells, *Economics and World Power*, 418.
12. Gary Burtless, Robert Z. Lawrence, Robert E. Litan, and Robert Shapiro, *Globaphobia: Confronting Fears about Open Trade* (Washington, DC: Brookings Institution Press, 1998), 1.
13. North American Integration and Development Center, http://naid.sppsr.ucla.edu.
14. The NAFTA Scam, http://www.uniteunion.org/reclaim/politicalarchive/nafta/nafta.html, p. 1, 2002.
15. Ibid., pp. 1–7.
16. Mobilization for Global Justice, http://www. a16.org, p. 2, 2002.
17. Edward Goldsmith, "Development as Colonialism," in *The Case against the Global Economy and for a Turn toward the Local*, ed. Jerry Mander and Edward Goldsmith (San Francisco: Sierra Club Books, 1996), 253.
18. Tony Clark, "Mechanisms of Corporate Rule," in *The Case against the Global Economy and for a Turn toward the Local*, ed. Jerry Mander and Edward Goldsmith (San Francisco: Sierra Club Books, 1996), 300.
19. *New York Times*, April 17, 2000.
20. *New York Times*, October 30, 1998.
21. David McCullough, *Truman* (New York: Simon and Schuster, 1992; Touchstone Books, 1993), 562.

3 Technology

"Technology drives globalization" is an oft-repeated phrase used by journalists and writers. It reflects the widespread belief that technological advances, particularly those related to "Information Technology," have made possible the vast growth of international commerce that brought forth the world-integrated economy. One of the best-sellers on globalization, *A Future Perfect* by John Micklethwait and Adrian Wooldridge, describes technology as one of the major components responsible for globalization. They regard it as a striking force that promotes freedom because it "gives people the power to weave connections all over the world. Technology allows people to escape," they continue, "from the tyranny of place."[1]

The average person associates computers with the technology of globalization, and understandably so, because of their use in transferring data and information. Rapid communications are indeed vital to an integrated economy, but other elements of technology are required, too. Transportation, whether by ship, air, rail, or truck, depends on an infrastructure of roads, highways, warehouses, and wharves. Refrigerated storage must be available for perishable goods. Communication satellites rely on the science of rocketry to put them in orbit. A vast array of technical advances and developments that support and reinforce each other are essential for globalized commerce and business.

There can be no date of origin for global technology, because it represents the culmination of centuries of innovation and experience. Each step rests on the one below it. The new advances of the last half-century have created the opportunities for large corporations to expand their markets onto an international field, giving rise to transnationals, which coordinate and organize various technologies for the sake of profit. Entrepreneurs and skilled managers strive to develop technologies for tapping new markets. They compete in a cycle of research, use, and replacement, all of which accelerate the use of and dependence on technology.

The newly arrived status of the world economy, or globalization, was the result of trade arrangements, the Cold War, technological innovations, and various supplemental impacting factors such as management and fresh sources of capital. For technology, a tidal wave of advancement since 1945 was brought about by several conditions. World War II stimulated research among the powers on both sides, so that at war's end there existed a new appreciation and respect for research and technology. German progress in rocketry and gas turbine engines and American breakthroughs in nuclear physics exemplified the war's impact. The United States and the Soviet Union put German scientists to work on their own rocket and missile projects as early as 1945, and their efforts served as the foundation of the space exploration of the latter twentieth century. Other examples of war-induced innovation included the advances in aircraft for military and civilian purposes. Wartime research into electromagnetic waves led to the development of the radio telescope and X-ray telescope used in satellite communications. Many of the breakthroughs in technology that promoted globalization either originated or received critical stimuli during the war. Indeed, World War II was such a catalyst in research that it could be regarded as a signal point in the appreciation of and demand for new technology. The Cold War rivalry of the superpowers drove this technology forward.

In addition to the contributions of the war, the United States in 1945 stood poised for more technological innovation. There was a pent-up demand for homes and consumer goods as Americans wanted to recover from the ills and sacrifices imposed by the hardship of the past generation. Companies looked forward to peacetime profits and the opportunities to expand. Because labor had a strong work ethic and the business class had a profit motive, these two forces created a cooperative spirit emphasizing growth and activity. Along with the determination to succeed, the country had other resources: raw materials, capital for investment, a federal policy committed to full employment, an intact infrastructure, a strong agricultural and industrial base, and institutions of higher education ready and willing to engage in research. And rooted in the business-managerial class was a mind-set of entrepreneurism that saw technology as a means to growth and success.

All of these assets were unleashed with the return from war of veterans in 1945, and the result was a robust economy with low inflation. The population explosion known as the baby boom reinforced the economy and improved even more the atmosphere for investment, research, and innovation. When the United States came out of the war, it had great advantages over other developed countries and set a course for itself directed toward progress and improvement. This American culture based on the anticipation of a bright future was highly conducive to technological advancement.

One innovation critical to globalization was jet aircraft. They made possible the speedy transfer of people and cargoes on an international basis. The Germans and British began developing military jets during World War II, but it was not until the latter 1950s and early 1960s that jet travel became common. The U.S. airline industry had a fleet of piston-engine DC-3s and DC-4s at the end of the war, but research to develop larger and faster planes began immediately. Military fighter jets went into operation during the Korean War, but not until 1959 did the Boeing Corporation introduce the first-generation jet airliner, the 707. During the 1960s another generation of jets went on the market when Boeing introduced the 727.

A spectacular development in transcontinental flight came with the Concorde, a supersonic passenger craft built in the 1960s as a joint venture by the British and French. The Concorde reduced transatlantic flights from eight to three hours. Despite its speed, the Concorde had little impact on air travel due to cost, but Boeing's 747 "jumbo jets," introduced in 1969, reduced the price of airfare to such an extent that it encouraged American tourism abroad. Flights across the Atlantic and Pacific were regularly scheduled; one-day travel to London, Paris, Tokyo, and other cities was possible without changing planes or making stops. In 1975, U.S.-scheduled airlines posted 5,912,000 passengers on international flights, but that figure grew to 24,513,000 by 1998.[2]

As stated by one authority, "Tourism has grown significantly since the creation of the commercial airline industry and the advent of the jet airplane in the 1950s."[3] In fact, tourism had become the world's largest single industry by the early 1990s and employed more persons than any other. International tourism had further global impact, but it rested fundamentally on jet travel. Air freight also grew with the development of jets, giving rise to the rapid transport of consumer goods and perishable foods as well as fast delivery of medicines and relief after natural disasters. Jets exemplified the new technological development that made possible the new integrated world economy.

Other means of transportation contributed, but their technological breakthroughs had occurred prior to World War II. Starting in the 1950s, however, the railroad and trucking industries combined to develope the "piggyback" method of hauling freight, a system known as "containerization." Full truck trailers are raised by dockside cranes from the cargo holds of ships and loaded onto flatbed railcars for their last trip, where only a quick haul takes them to their final destination. American agriculture depends heavily on the export market, and commodities such as wheat, cotton, soybeans, and corn ride the rails to seaports. Rail traffic, not as new or as glamorous as jet travel, serves as a fundamental mode of transportation for international commerce. A similar pattern is evident with ships, which have promoted globalization for centuries. The oil tanker, a new development since 1945, was designed to carry the oil needed due to its growing use for energy and the need for developed countries to import it. In 1970 the United States required only 483,000,000 barrels of imported oil, but by 2000 it imported 3,178,000,000 barrels.[4]

Improvements in agricultural technology and advances in the preservation and storage of food were more steps toward the world's integrated economy. Production of food and fiber went up around the world not only in developing countries but also in rich nations such as the United States that started practicing high-yield agriculture. For the global market, the result was an increase in production over the last half-century, which provided more food for the world's burgeoning population. Mechanization accounted for the increases in the developed countries, but the most dramatic improvements came in poorer countries due to the use of better varieties and strains of plants. Advances in rice farming raised the yields per acre and accounted for the emergence of Thailand, Pakistan, India, China, Vietnam, and the United States as the leaders in rice exports. A similar development occurred with wheat. The United States, Canada, and Western Europe continued to supply the bulk of export wheat, which came as a result of mechanization and improved varieties. China, which exported rice, had to import wheat; the reverse process occurred with Italy. Corn remained a principal export crop for the United States, which sold over 35,877 metric tons in 1994 compared with China, its closest competitor, which sold 8,740 metric tons in the world market the same year.

Advances in the varieties of these food crops partly accounted for their greater production. Insect control through a system known as Integrated Pest Management (IPM), which was developed in the United States, reduced crop losses to insects. So impressive was the greater production of food that it came to be known as the Green Revolution, and it freed people, at least in some countries, for industrial and manufacturing jobs. The ensured food supply, wrought by scientific research and the application of practical knowledge, released manpower and capital for technical development.

It is obvious that many of the technologies promoting globalization were commonplace prior to World War II and continued to be utilized for the rest of the century. In one case, however, a new one grew almost entirely in the latter twentieth century and bore directly upon globalization: information technology, or IT. As one writer stated in 1996, "A new economy has emerged in the last two decades on a worldwide scale. I call it informational and global to identify its fundamental distinctive features and to emphasize their intertwining."[5] This advance reached deeply into the world economy and culture by affecting business and manufacturers, military operations, educational and cultural institutions, and the daily lives of a large segment of the world's population. "It is possible to foresee a time, not many decades hence," wrote an analyst for the World Resources Institute, "when nearly every village on the planet will be connected to information networks via global wireless and satellite links."[6]

From a solely technical point of view, the communications revolution arguably started with the invention of the telephone in 1876, but during World War II the first computer and transistor were invented. Each of IT's three principal components—computers, telecommunications, and microelectronics—came a short time later. In 1947, Bell Laboratories in New Jersey invented the transistor that made possible the structuring of data between machines through semiconductors or chips. Advances with semiconductors came in the 1950s at Texas Instruments and Fairchild Semiconductors, which enabled semiconductors to be produced as miniatures. In 1957, Texas Instruments developed the integrated circuit that initiated large-scale production of microelectronic items at reduced cost. In 1971, Intel invented the microprocessor, which broadened the availability and use of various devices such as computers that could process information. With this breakthrough it became possible to implant many circuits on a single chip, and the speed of processing and transmitting data leapt forward. By the mid-1990s, computers were able to process information over 500 times faster than they did using the chips of 1971. Further improvements in miniaturization of chips and their falling price enabled manufacturers to implant them in household items such as microwave ovens and dishwashers as well as in tools, heating and cooling systems, and a host of other common conveniences. Devices relying on computer chips became a regular feature of daily life in the United States.

The greatest impact of microchips came through the computer, whose evolution ran parallel with the digital processing of information and data. Early progress was made during World War II when the British managed to decipher German coded messages with their Colossus, and the Germans had their Z-3 to make calculations. Engineers at the University of Pennsylvania developed the ENIAC, which had over 18,000 vacuum tubes and took up as much space as a basketball court. Engineers quickly followed in 1951 with the UNIVAC, the first commercial computer. It relied on mercury tubes through which impulses were sent. These two giant machines belonged to the first generation of computers.

In the 1950s the second-generation computers incorporated the use of transistors, which were superior to vacuum tubes for processing information. Transistors enabled manufacturers to produce computers that were smaller, less expensive, and more reliable. Even higher speeds and smaller size became available with the third generation, which utilized miniaturized transistors and integrated circuits. Still higher-speed computers with more reliability were possible, and soon the fourth-generation computers became available. This last generation furnished more speed and the ability to handle more complex data. Engineers achieved this capability by installing more transistors and circuitry on a single chip. Such progress enabled manufacturers to use fewer chips and thereby reduce the price for consumers. Herein lies much of the significance of the breakthroughs in chip technology: the ability of industry to manufacture computers at a reasonable cost. Other technological advances were needed, however, to make possible international communications.

Computer and transistor technology alone would not suffice to explain the new state of global communications. The communications satellites launched in the mid-1960s increased the number of telephone messages and television transmissions that could be sent simultaneously. From a mere 240 simultaneous messages with the Intelsat 1, sent into orbit in 1965, the Intelsat 8 transmitted over 22,000 telephone messages and three television channels at the same time. Other satellites served regions in Europe, North America, and Latin America. "In this respect," wrote an economic geographer, "the key element is the linking together of computer technologies with information-transmission technologies over vast differences."[7] The Internet still needed another advance in order for it to be within the reach of the general population. That step came in 1978.

In that year two students at the University of Chicago invented the modem, which relied on telephone lines. They made further improvements during the next year and developed the ability to conduct on-line computer discussions. At that point the ARPANET, the information system controlled by the military, served as the only avenue of networking, but now discussion and the exchange of information became possible with personal computers outside the ARPANET. From this technical achievement came the Bulletin Board Systems that required only a personal computer with a modem and telephone lines. Almost suddenly, it seemed, worldwide communication became possible, and as corporations saw the benefits and advantages of the Internet, the National Science Foundation made it available to the networks already established by international companies. The Internet grew rapidly as subservers climbed aboard.

For networking, switches or nodes were necessary to transmit data quickly and efficiently from one source to another. Fiber optics increased the number of transmissions that could be carried on a cable. A phone cable could carry about fifty messages at one time, but an optic fiber could carry 85,000.[8] These various advances and others made possible the creation of a "network society," an interlinked system of communications and data processing that brought about the revolution in information technology. The establishment of this network created in turn the opportunity for businesses to expand their operations globally or to become transnationals. "Technological changes, particularly in the space-shrinking technologies of transport and communications," stated one account, helped "to make possible the internationalization of economic activity and the development and geographical spread of transnational corporations."[9]

Transnationals vary in their methods of operations, so that no precise definition would fit every one, but without the technological developments in communications and the infrastructure of trade, they could not function. Nearly all of them exhibit characteristics that are common. They generally operate in various countries and regions of the world through the processes of production, coordination, and distribution. In some cases they own the methods of production—that is, the factories that manufacture their goods—but others shy away from production. Nearly all have a central headquarters that coordinates and organizes their activities around the globe. Transnationals pay close attention to consumer taste and trends and thereby devote resources to marketing research. They design goods with the consumer in mind and may draw up specifications for production. An important component of their operations is capital—they must raise large sums to carry out their operations. To do so requires the transfer of capital across national boundaries, known as capital flow. These flows often move from bank to bank, say, from New York to London or from San Francisco to Tokyo.

A transnational corporation may typically have the same product manufactured in several countries, which requires a great degree of coordination. It will have to arrange contracts, ship various components to and from the site of production, keep up with its own inventories, and maintain a supply chain. As goods and services move across borders, the transnational will have to deal with import and export regulations, licensing requirements, tariffs, and currency exchanges. A flow of information between the various plants and offices of the company occurs on a steady basis, following a twenty-four-hour international clock. The rise and fall of currencies can affect, for example, the profit margin, so a transnational must maintain constant vigilance over international currency markets and be able to act almost instantly. These international transactions obviously depend on a global network of communications and fast transportation. Without the technological capabilities inherent in the developed countries, transnationals could not exist.

Still another technology that accounts for the world-integrated economy, as well as a growing sense of global culture, is television. The development of television stretched back to the 1880s, but in 1923, when Vladimir Zworykin, a Russian-born physicist working for Westinghouse, invented the iconoscope, a major step took place. In 1930, Philo Farnsworth invented a scanning system that made pictures suitable for home viewing. In 1941 the Federal Communications Commission (FCC) authorized the first commercial station, WNBT in New York, which broadcast fifteen hours per week. World War II slowed down development, but it quickly resumed in 1945, so that by 1948 there were thirty-six stations on the air and about 1 million sets in American homes. From 1948 through 1952 the FCC delayed further expansion due to the Korean War, but television grew exponentially during the next decade, until by the mid-1960s sets were commonplace in U.S. households and throughout much of Europe. A slower pace of growth occurred in developing or poorer countries, but by the 1990s television sets were becoming more common everywhere.

International broadcasting began in 1965 when Intelsat 1, the first commercial communications satellite, was placed over the Atlantic. It transmitted television broadcasts from the United States to Europe. In 1967 more Intelsat satellites were placed into orbit, one over the Atlantic Ocean and two over the Pacific Ocean. All together, these satellites made television broadcasting possible over two-thirds of the globe. This new development enabled another technological feat to have a profound impact on the world's population. In 1969, when Neil Armstrong made the first moon landing, 600 million people in fifty countries on six continents watched it on television. By 2002 television viewing was common around the world except in the poorest and most remote areas.

Television's impact on global culture and behavior is staggering. For one thing, Third World inhabitants in remote areas are able to observe the lifestyle of people in the most advanced countries along with the material well-being and political and social practices regarded as a common right in developed societies. "Today, it is television which has the most dramatic impact on people's awareness and perception of worlds beyond their own direct experience," wrote one global analyst.[10]

Still another technological advance with global implications is telephony, or the use of mobile or cell phones. Inexpensive and small, the mobile phone enables a person to connect with anyone possessing a telephone. Although the employment of these devices for international transactions is a fraction of their total use, they nonetheless have broadened the general awareness of their users, particularly those in remote areas. Developing countries have the most to gain because mobile phone communication enables them to avoid the lack of a fixed telephone infrastructure, which discourages the interest of outside investors. Countries such as South Africa, Botswana, Zimbabwe, Gabon, and Uganda had altogether nearly 2 million mobile phone users by 2001.[11] How far all these innovations will go remains unknown, for according to one assessment, "The emergence of a new electronic communication system characterized by its global reach, its integration of all communication media, and its potential interactivity is changing and will forever change our culture."[12]

Transnationals such as Nike and Coca-Cola now advertise on international television in order to maintain a global market. Foreign sales became an important component of their profitability whenever the U.S. economy experienced a downturn. Some international corporations even have budgets and economic operations larger than the national budgets of small countries.[13] Without television and its global reach, they would have much less impact and influence in the integrated market. Transnationals drive the international economy, but they depend on the new technologies developed since 1945. In this sense, technology is essential to globalization and explains the common belief that technology drives globalization.

With the advantage of the global information network, transnationals manage to exert influence in both domestic and international markets. They practice efficiency of production, for example, by keeping inventories to a minimum, by knowing the latest market conditions, by routing supplies and finished products through the most efficient channels, and by custom designing and manufacturing products for a variety of markets around the world. The greater efficiency and advantages of large-volume production generally reduce the price of their goods, thus making them available to a large number of people. A transnational dealing in agricultural commodities that stays abreast of world weather conditions and food harvests can anticipate trends in prices. That information alone provides an advantage over smaller companies.

Information technology, upon which transnationals depend, has inherent flaws and drawbacks. For example, protecting intellectual property has become a matter of concern. Data, inventions, creative works, and various forms of information embedded in documents and images can be pilfered in foreign lands. In high-tech piracy, computer software, costly to design and produce, is easily duplicated. Pharmaceutical companies likewise lose control over the production of drugs developed in their laboratories. Serious questions arise over the practice of transnationals shifting production into developing countries with low-skilled labor, and union labor is hostile toward those corporations for that reason. As the technology of computers and informational services expands and becomes more complex, unskilled labor falls behind. Generally this condition is worst in Third World countries, but poorly educated and untrained workers in the United States and Europe have also suffered loss of employment. Another concern is the loss of privacy by individuals whose financial and personal records fall into the hands of sales companies or even criminals. Concerns have arisen over the ability of authoritarian governments to exercise control over their citizens by gaining access to their records.

International crime paralleled the rise of transnationals. Drug cartels centered in South America or Asia transport illicit substances into the United States and Europe through the same means of modern transport used by legitimate corporations. As nations ease restrictions on border inspections for the sake of trade, drugs cross borders more easily. By taking advantage of information technology and the communications revolution, sophisticated criminal organizations conceal their financial transactions, estimated at $500 billion per year, when about $1 trillion in capital flows around the world each year.[14] International cyberspace enables drug traffickers, arms dealers, and pornographers to act on a global scale and enjoy less risk of detection as they conceal their operations in the mass of daily transactions in the world economy.

A major theme of globalization is the lag of poorer countries in the Third World that have not benefited from the integrated economy because the great bulk of international commercial transactions occur among developed countries, which receive the greatest benefits. Undeveloped countries have been left behind, or at least they have not benefited at the same level and rate. This condition is a consequence of the ruthless nature of capitalism: corporations invest capital and develop markets in those areas where they anticipate success, and they naturally regard the developed societies as a logical choice. To choose market areas in poor or developing countries that promise little or no success would endanger the solvency of a firm and could eventually drive it out of business. Technologies, as a consequence, tend to follow other technologies, leaving the undeveloped regions alone and isolated from the flow of information. The innovations of global technology thereby promote the economic advancement of developed societies while ignoring the poorer ones. A gap in the standard of living emerges between them, and antiglobalization critics put the blame for this widening gap on the transnationals. Poorer nations seek help from international institutions such as the United Nations and the World Bank, or they try to attract foreign investment in electronic information systems.

Rapid movement of capital across borders, sometimes to the detriment of small countries, became possible only with the technological revolution of the latter twentieth century, which includes the vast web of communications, information exchanges, and data processing and computation that is described as the "network society." This network or infrastructure of communications has become inseparably linked with world capital flows, currency exchanges, trade surpluses and deficits, nontariff barriers, and efforts by international organizations such as the WTO to regulate world trade.

In a strong and healthy economy, availability of capital is a necessary condition, so capital flowing into and out of a country has much importance. Transnationals account for a large portion of the flows, but governments and organizations such as the IMF and the World Bank account for a large portion. In 2001 the IMF loaned over $8 billion to Argentina in hopes of averting a financial collapse of its economy. Private interests and investors focus their attention on interest rates because they want to put their money into those banks offering the best rate, but the political stability and tax policies of a country also affect their decisions. During the 1990s, the United States attracted considerable capital because of its robust economy as compared with the economies of Europe and Japan. Since capital flows depend on opportunity and safety, which work to the advantage of developed nations, poorer or developing countries may offer incentives to attract investors.

Closely related to capital flows are currency exchanges, which also increased with the new technologies of global communications. Exchanges refer to the buying and selling of currencies because of either their constant rise and fall in value or the need to convert holdings in foreign currencies accumulating from trade. Under the Bretton Woods system established in 1944, worldwide currencies were pegged to the dollar, but after the "Nixon shocks" of 1971, when the dollar started floating on the international market, currency exchanges increased since a common denominator no longer existed. Because a currency's value depends on the soundness of the economy it represents, the more prized currencies nearly always belong to the most developed countries. For this reason, the American dollar, German mark, Japanese yen, British pound, and Swiss franc are the most traded and popular currencies. Industries generating much of the exchange in currency are automobiles, electronics, agriculture, and textiles, but large banks usually handle the exchanges. Tourism also brings about a large accumulation of foreign currencies that must be converted. Hoping to profit from variations in exchange rates, speculators buy and sell currencies, trying to practice the old axiom of "buy low and sell high." The fast and voluminous transfer of capital constitutes one of the new characteristics of the global economy, so much so that "international financial flows and foreign currency exchanges," according to one authority, "now dwarf the value of international trade in goods."[15]

Only economists and financiers seem to understand the intricate procedures involved in determining currency exchange rates. In order to be as accurate and thorough as possible in setting rates, economists rely on data from a variety of factors such as consumer preferences, trade policies, productivity, capital flows, and inflation rates. In 1986, *The Economist* magazine introduced "Burgernomics" as a whimsical effort conducted each year to follow currency values around the world. By 2000, McDonald's operated restaurants in 120 countries, so the price of a Big Mac could theoretically be set in one at a value equal to the price in other countries. If Burgernomics worked perfectly, the price of a Big Mac would be the same everywhere. By studying these prices, it would be possible to determine if currencies were over- or undervalued. While *The Economist* acknowledged the flaws in the use of "MacCurrencies," it showed that on a long-term basis Burgernomics has been fairly accurate.[16]

Trade deficits affect currency values. If American consumers show, for example, a preference for foreign goods and cause the United States to increase its trade deficit, the value of the dollar will fall and exchange rates will have to be adjusted. If the United States should develop a trade surplus, the value of the dollar will increase, requiring another adjustment. Economists refer to this dimension of trade as the balance of payments.

Transactions in international trade are not unique to the last fifty years, but the new technologies of communications increased the ease and efficiency of conducting business on a global scale and brought an increase in the number of transnationals. Over 37,000 transnational corporations existed by the 1990s and they had 170,000 foreign affiliates.[17] A critical outgrowth of their activities has been financial services, which refer to services provided for businesses or consumers. Examples include banks, data processing firms, advertising and marketing agencies, tourism, education, and consulting and communications companies. The world's integrated economy relies on these services, which in turn rely on communications. In this respect the revolution in information technology is vital to globalization. For the industrialized countries with an infrastructure of electricity, telephones, satellite communications, and other elements of IT, the new technology can easily be put to use and thereby enhance their society economically and culturally. In a competitive global market, investors and transnationals will naturally prefer to conduct business there and avoid the developing countries with smaller markets; therefore, "90 percent of TNCs are headquartered in the advanced capitalist states."[18] Thus, another complex element explains the widening gap between the rich and poor nations, with personal incomes and levels of gross national product spreading further apart. So while some societies enjoy the benefits of the new technologies, others continue to fall further behind. Because of the rapid development of the information technologies in the last quarter-century, the differences between the two have accelerated.

The rising importance of financial services was responsible for much of the difference. Until the 1970s most of the foreign investments went into manufacturing and industrial development, but with the rise of the new technologies the lion's share of such investments started going into services, particularly financial services. Some states in Southeast Asia, known as the "Tiger economies," managed to improve their financial well-being, thanks to the growth of international tourism made possible by the development of jet transport.[19] They also took advantage of their pool of cheap labor, which enticed investors to build assembly plants. East Asia quickly became an attractive growth region in which the future seemed rosy and assuring—an investor euphoria developed there known as the "Golden Scenario." Capital flowed into the Tiger economies, and especially into Thailand, when it pegged its currency to the U.S. dollar.

In 1997, however, East Asia went into a sharp downturn when investors and speculators anticipated a hike in interest rates in Japan. Currency reserves in Thailand were already dangerously low due to the country's trade deficit. Investors lost faith in the market and started pulling out their money. The central bank of Thailand started buying dollars to stem the outflow of capital, but speculators smelled blood and "attacked" the baht, the Thai currency. Thus, a currency crisis erupted and spread to other Tiger countries as speculators attacked their currencies. As the Asian countries sought outside help from organizations such as the IMF, confidence in their economies slipped lower. The Asian crisis affected economies around the world. American agriculture, for example, experienced a drop in exports. This fall, known as the "Asian flu," eroded some of the strength of the American and European economies.

From the beginning of the boom through the bust in the Tiger economies, technology played a key role. Instant communications and computer capabilities enabled investors to quickly analyze opportunities and transfer large amounts of capital into banks there. By the same token, they were able to follow the financial markets in Japan and quickly move their funds there. Other investors were able to note the trend in capital flows and followed suit, so the Thai currency weakness set off a frenzy of capital withdrawals. A domino effect ensued among East Asian countries, and the Tiger economies soon lost their bloom. Technology did not cause the East Asian economies to falter, but it doubtless enhanced and intensified the rapidity of their rise and fall.

Even though some regions of the world have not experienced the benefits of globalization, technology moves so fast that some hurdles may be overcome. African countries generally have little infrastructure for telephones, so they started to rely on wireless mobile telephones, thus enabling them to "leapfrog [over] an obstacle to development." With the sudden availability of telephones, a "quiet revolution" brought a new sense of power to the people in semi-isolated areas. Already the ruling political parties have felt the pressure of a democratic surge, all of which rested on the use of fast communication.[20]

When the new information technologies first appeared and began to spread during the latter twentieth century, there was great optimism about their anticipated impact on trade, art and culture, and even freedom of the individual. It was widely assumed that with Internet connections, individuals or companies could work in one country and offer services to clients beyond their national borders. This expectation came true to the extent that transnationals established overseas data banks and processing centers for handling various accounts. In Africa, for example, health maintenance organizations (HMOs) based in the United States have set up processing centers to handle claims made by insured customers. Africans with elementary computer skills found employment, which brought them an improved standard of living.[21] Satellites make possible such operations, illustrating again how the world's integrated economy depends on the technologies of borderless communications.

A new concern arose, however, that may impose restrictions on the flow of information across borders. In 2000 a French court ruled that an international Internet server could not offer Nazi artifacts on its auction website because Nazi items such as medals, uniforms, and other paraphernalia may not, by French law, be put on public display. Defenders of free speech and the freedom of the Internet, exemplified by the Center of Democracy and Technology, protested on the grounds that any limitations on use of the Internet could lead to even more severe restrictions.

Courts in two other European countries handed down similar rulings, and the combination of these decisions stirred concern that censorship may be developing. Internet servers might adjust the content of their websites, so the concern went, on a nation-by-nation basis. A new technology under development, known as geolocation, would enable servers to segregate the markets for receiving material. China already blocks some websites from outside vendors. If unfettered, restrictions could become endless so that cities and small towns could regulate material content. In 2002 this question of restriction remained in the courts, but it suggested that the original intention of having an international flow of information free of all restraints may not survive. As summarized by *The Economist*, "As the Internet's architecture changes and becomes more complex, with the addition of services like filtering and geolocation, the idea that the Internet is beyond the reach of local laws and government regulation looks less and less tenable."[22]

The technology of globalization had many social effects. It was considered a force in the downfall of the Soviet Union because it enabled anti-Communist forces to communicate and organize. It opened a new vista in American education with the development of on-line courses taught over the Internet; universities in the United States now commonly offer courses to students in Europe, South America, and Asia that are taught through cyberspace. Manufacturing companies experienced a major step forward with the related use of computers as global communications permitted them to enhance their control of distribution, to minimize inventories, and to practice computer-integrated manufacturing (CIM), which leads to more precise production techniques. Efficiency in production reduced waste and energy use. High-tech factories equipped with robotic machines and linked to a global net of suppliers, distributors, and clients reduced manpower needs.

For some workers, this change meant a loss of jobs, especially for the low-skilled. Just as the impact of the Industrial Revolution brought much upheaval and adjustment to the lives of skilled craftsmen, the revolution in information technology and computer-integrated manufacturing displaced workers even if it removed much of the toil and drudgery of assembly-line labor. This development accounted for much of the job losses in heavy industries and the rise of services.

When connected with globalization, technology became a contentious subject in regard to climate change, or global warming. Scientific evidence showed that the Earth's average daily temperature had climbed about 1 degree Fahrenheit over the last 100 years and that future increases might occur. A condition known as the "greenhouse effect" developed from the release of gases into the atmosphere, with the most damaging coming from carbon dioxide, methane, and nitrous oxide. These gases became trapped in the atmosphere and caused a rise in the temperature. According to the Environmental Protection Agency (EPA), average sea levels rose 10 to 12 inches in the last 100 years. The greater use of machines, electronics, and other examples of industrialization and technological development accounted for the appearance of gases, and scientists nearly always blamed the use of fossil fuels in automobiles, trucks, homes, and industry for worsening the greenhouse effect. Agriculture also accounted for a portion of the gases.

With only a slight increase of from 1 to 2 degrees, parts of Earth's polar caps would melt and raise the planet's sea level another 2 feet, enough to inundate some portions of coastal areas. Thousands of square miles of Earth's inhabitable land might be lost, with irreversible consequences, and bring major population shifts. So staggering are the implications of these predictions that many people apart from environmentalists believe that waiting for further and conclusive evidence would be foolish. In 1997 the United States along with 166 other nations entered into the Kyoto Agreement specifying that the ratifying countries would be legally bound to reduce emission levels within their jurisdiction. At least fifty-five countries had to ratify the agreement before it would go into effect.

By 2000, global warming had become a matter of popular concern in the United States. In that year Democratic presidential candidate Albert Gore urged the country to accept the scientific evidence as sufficient reason to initiate action for reducing pollutants in the atmosphere. In 1992 he had published *Earth in the Balance: Ecology and the Human Spirit*, in which he accepted the concept of global warming. As a candidate for the White House, he made it an issue in the election campaign of 2000.

For globalization the campaign had significance. Gore accepted global warming as a threat and proposed U.S. ratification of the Kyoto Agreement. He opposed oil drilling in the Arctic National Wildlife Refuge and urged adoption of tax credits for corporations willing to improve energy efficiency in homes, automobiles, and electrical power plants. In the campaign, Gore clearly stood out as the candidate more likely to impose environmental controls.[23]

George W. Bush, the winner of the election, took a moderate stance. He recognized the legitimacy of global warming but opposed the Kyoto Agreement. For Bush, the scientific evidence was insufficient to warrant the imposition of legally binding controls on American manufacturers and corporations. "It's an issue that we need to take very seriously," he stated. "I don't think we know the solutions to global warming yet and I don't think we've got all the facts before we make decisions."[24] Bush supported limited drilling in the Arctic Wildlife Refuge and new exploration for oil and natural gas.

Gore's sense of urgency and Bush's call for caution reflected the complex nature of environmentalism in the new global economy. No one could deny the presence of smog, acid rain, and contaminated water. Deforestation and the increased use of fossil fuels associated with industrialization explained the temperature rise in the nineteenth and most of the twentieth century, but it remained unclear if human activity accounted for it. Of the ten hottest years on record, nine occurred between 1987 and 1997. Some scientists attributed the changes to natural weather patterns such as the Pacific Ocean current called El Niño. In 1995 the United Nations, through its Intergovernmental Panel on Climate Change (IPCC), reported that evidence for a decisive conclusion was insufficient.[25]

In the context of globalization, the issue of the environment related to the impact of pollution controls on the competitive effectiveness of American industry in the international economy. Globalists and free-traders generally endorsed environmentalism and the efforts to reduce damage to the wilderness and other elements of nature. They warned, however, that since the U.S. economy faced severe competition, regulations must be imposed cautiously because the United States might require stiffer antipollution practices than its competitors and thereby give them an unfair advantage. Enthusiasm for environmentalism also tended to come from developed nations, while the poorer ones sought to maximize economic growth. The latter viewed efforts to mandate environmental regulations as an imperialistic tactic by rich nations to drive out competition from the Third World and "lessen the opportunity for less developed nations to grow."[26] The impasse only worsened the situation, since U.S. importers were able to buy cheaply from foreign sources whose production costs were lower.

Proposals to encourage multinationals to reduce their pollution output included government subsidies and special tariffs on goods manufactured in countries with lenient regulations. Subsidies and tariffs strike at the heart of free trade, however, because tariff wars might erupt, and subsidies already constituted a barrier to further trade as seen in the case of agriculture. In 1999, when President Bill Clinton spoke to the WTO meeting in Seattle, he urged the organization to find a way to incorporate standards for environmentalism into its operations.[27]

It is generally recognized that damage and destruction of natural resources occurred daily around the world as the result of normal economic activity. Individuals seeking to earn a livelihood, such as the farmers in South America destroying rain forests to gain cropland or transnationals drawing oil and other nonrenewable resources from the earth, had an impact on the environment. Antiglobalists usually targeted the multinational corporations as the chief culprits. Major offenders included oil conglomerates, paper and pulp mills, large-scale farmers and ranchers, electric utility companies, commercial fisheries, logging firms, and various other corporations extracting or using Earth's resources. Governments were also the target of criticism and protests.

At the foundation of the problem, according to environmentalists, lay the philosophy of economic growth. Increased trade and development brought global industrialization, which heightened pollution and ecological damage. One environmentalist stated this position: "Clearly, there is no way of protecting our environment within the context of a global 'free trade' economy committed to continued economic growth and hence to increasing the harmful impact of our activities on an already fragile environment."[28]

Technology is critical to globalization because without it there would be no integrated world economy. The advances made since 1945 pushed forward the ability of countries to engage in trade and commerce even though the history of innovation stretched far back into time. The innovations since 1970, however, seem to be the most relevant because they relate to communications and computer technology. Large corporations took advantage of these new tools and expanded their operations as transnationals whose activities did much to advance globalization. Because technology also had an impact on the traditional methods of production, service industries grew. The social and political effects of global technology are still unfolding, especially in poorer countries where people demand its benefits.

NOTES

1. John Micklethwait and Adrian Wooldridge, *A Future Perfect: The Essentials of Globalization* (New York: Crown, 2000), 33; *New York Times*, July 20, 2000.
2. Table I-38, Air Passenger Travel Departures from the United States to Selected Foreign Countries (Thousands), http://www.bts.gov/btsprod/nts/ch1_web/1-38.htm.
3. William Theobold, ed., *Global Tourism: The Next Decade* (Oxford, Eng.: Butterworth-Heinemann, 1995), 1.
4. U.S. Census Bureau, *Statistical Abstract of the United States: 2000*, 120th ed. (Washington, DC, 2000), 591.
5. Manuel Castells, *The Rise of the Network Society* , vol. 1 of *The Information Age: Economy, Society, and Culture* (Oxford, Eng.: Blackwell, 1996), 66.
6. Allen Hammond, *Which World? Scenarios for the 21st Century: Global Destinies, Regional Choices* (Washington, DC: Island Press, 2000), 36.
7. Dicken, *Global Shift*, 155.
8. Castells, *Network Society*, 46.
9. Dicken, *Global Shift*, 178.
10. Ibid., 158.
11. *Newsweek* (August 27, 2001): 32.
12. Castells, *Network Society*, 329.
13. LaFeber, *Michael Jordan and the New Global Capitalism*, 56–57.
14. Hammond, *Which World? Scenarios for the 21st Century*, 105–6.
15. Dicken, *Global Shift*, 399.
16. Big Mac Currencies, http://www.economist.com/markets/bigmac/displaystory. cfm?story_id:305167, 2002.
17. R. J. Johnston, Peter J. Taylor, and Michael J. Watts, eds., *Geographies of Global Change: Remapping the World in the Late Twentieth Century* (Oxford, Eng.: Blackwell, 1996), 13.

18. Ibid.
19. François Vellas, "Strategic Marketing in the Air Transport Sector," in *The International Marketing of Travel and Tourism: A Strategic Approach*, ed. François Vellas and Lionel Becherel (New York: St. Martin's Press, 1999), 215–17.
20. *Newsweek* (August 27, 2001): 32.
21. *New York Times*, May 8, 2001.
22. *The Economist* (August 11, 2001): 20.
23. Issues 2001, http://www.issues2000.org/Celeb/Al Gore Environment. html, p. 6, 2002.
24. Issues 2001, http://www.issues2000.org/Celeb/George W Bush Environment.html, p. 7, 2002.
25. J. R. McNeill, *An Environmental History of the Twentieth Century World: Something New under the Sun* (New York: W. W. Norton, 2000), 110.
26. Carbaugh, *International Economics*, 101.
27. Ibid., 102; *New York Times*, December 2, 1999.
28. Goldsmith, "Global Trade and the Environment," 91.

4

The United States and World Markets

The globalization of the United States rested in great part on its activity in world markets. As soon as World War II ended, industries resumed their prewar activities and expanded them in the succeeding decades, although some sectors, such as services, only acquired global significance toward the end of the century. In some instances, the federal government and industries worked together, as seen in agriculture. In other cases, corporations, relying less on government assistance, took advantage of the opportunities presented by new technologies and sources of capital and expanded their markets around the world. The national interests of the United States and the desires of private enterprise meshed together in regard to international trade, so that by 2002 the American economy relied heavily on the integrated world market. Transnationals played a key role, accounting for a large portion of the capital flows, construction of factories with long assembly lines, distribution infrastructure, and other elements essential for mass production and global marketing. For this achievement, they relied on instant communications, quick transport, computers, and modern managerial methods.[1] The point at which corporations exhibited characteristics as transnationals varied from one to another, but writers began to note their rising influence and power by the 1970s. According to one study, they were "ushering in a genuine world economy."[2] The globalizing effects of the broader American economy began, however, at the end of World War II, with agriculture in the lead.

Agriculture's dependence on world trade stretched far back into U.S. history, to such an extent that the reduction in farm exports after World War I came to be regarded as a major cause of the Great Depression. In 1945 agricultural and political leaders believed that restoration of the export market was imperative for the welfare of the country. The need to promote overseas markets for agriculture had always been a cornerstone of American trade policy and had enjoyed bipartisan support because farm income depended on exports. Trade agreements made in Washington nearly always reflected a deep concern for the interests of farmers and ranchers. For these reasons, agriculture ranked at the top of those American industries that had a globalizing effect on the world economy.

Immediately after World War II the United States sent food and fiber abroad for humanitarian reasons. The United Nations Relief and Rehabilitation Administration program, the Economic Cooperation Administration, and the Mutual Security Agency sent large shipments for civilian consumption into liberated areas, particularly to Germany and Japan. Britain purchased foodstuffs and cotton with a $3.6 billion loan from the U.S. government. Domestic consumption of food was high, too, so the postwar market and prices for agricultural commodities were strong, and during the Korean War (1950–1953), food prices in the United States were slightly inflationary. By the mid-1950s, however, surpluses began to return with the commodities of wheat, corn, cotton, dairy products, and other staples. Anxious to invigorate overseas sales, the federal government started a program in 1954, based on the Agricultural Trade and Development Act, known as P.L. 480 that sold commodities overseas for foreign currency.

The P.L. 480 program was intended to enable developing countries to purchase U.S. farm commodities even though they had no dollars or items for sale with which to acquire dollars. By accepting their currencies, the United States expanded its farm exports and also created an outlet for foreign aid and humanitarian relief. With the currencies received via P.L. 480, the United States in turn could purchase goods or spend them on such developmental activities as military or U.S. federal projects in those countries. The real goal, however, was to obtain a marketing foothold in nations with no regular trade exchange with the United States. This strategy succeeded in countries such as Brazil, South Korea, Japan, Taiwan, and Spain. From the humanitarian aspect, P.L. 480 provided food donations for famine or other emergencies. From the perspective of globalization, the program expanded farm exports into those international markets that were not already active trading partners. Thus, exports grew and American agricultural trade expanded.

Agricultural cooperatives were another arm of export trade. Consisting of farmers who wished to promote their own sales, both domestic and foreign, cooperatives entered into export agreements with overseas clients such as wholesale food companies and textile firms. Cooperatives shipped their commodities by ship, rail, and truck directly to overseas purchasers in a unilateral agreement. In 1980 cooperatives accounted for only about 7 percent of total U.S. grain sales but for nearly 50 percent of the export sales in fruits. Rice growers developed an extensive mechanism for exporting their product by acquiring their own port elevators and starting brand names such as Riceland and American Rice, Inc.[3]

Agriculture became a sensitive subject among the world's trading partners. Shortly after World War II, when foodstuffs were not plentiful, countries made little effort to protect their own domestic producers, but as the global economy recovered from the war, self-interest prevailed and restrictions on the export-import trade started to appear. A complex arrangement in agricultural trade developed, because even though the United States embraced free trade, it allowed domestic and export subsidies for farm interests. Other countries had similar practices, so that agriculture received special consideration when these countries conducted trade agreements. In the beginning of GATT negotiations in 1947, agricultural commodities traded on the same basis as industrial goods, but in 1955 the United States won concessions for imposing quotas on agricultural output, known as Section 22. During the Dillon Round of 1961, the European Community began to withdraw concessions, so agricultural commodities became increasingly exempt from the general practice of reducing barriers to trade.

Behind this practice was the desire to maintain domestic subsidy programs for farmers. GATT allowed its members to use quotas instead of tariffs when trading agricultural commodities. By the Uruguay Round in 1986, sharp differences existed between the three regional trading blocs—the United States, Europe, and Japan—over agriculture, which provoked some of the urgency to create a more encompassing body, the World Trade Organization, which replaced GATT in 1995. Progress on agricultural items still remained slow, and individual differences were sometimes resolved through settlements. In 1998 tariffs and quotas averaged about 40 percent on agricultural goods compared with about 10 percent on manufactured products.[4]

Since 1945 the growth in the international trade of agriculture grew by leaps and bounds. In 1998 about $456 billion in food and fiber traded around the world, more than three times the amount in the late 1970s.[5] Food consumption rose and costs fell on a per capita basis. In the United States, food generally accounted for about 15 percent of the cost of living. Certain developing countries had become major exporters of food and fiber: Brazil, Thailand, and China. By 1997, China replaced the United States as the largest grower of cotton, and the former Soviet republic of Uzbekistan became a notable producer. The United States used to dominate the world market in cotton, but the rise of competitors in the last fifty years eroded many of its advantages even though global consumption rose about 50 percent.[6] From a global perspective, food is plentiful, but shortages and famine still occur in particular locales, nearly always arising from extreme weather, problems in distribution, and political instability rather than short-falls in supply.

No trade item has as many global ramifications as agriculture. Crops necessary for human subsistence are grown almost everywhere, so that production in one country has the potential to affect prices through-out the international market. Countries anxious to emerge as an economic power nearly always begin by developing a strong agricultural base, which has more impact on the global stage. Policies adopted by countries to protect their farmers likewise have an impact on trade, restricting access to markets. Occasionally, outbreaks of disease in cattle or crop failures will reverberate around the globe. The outbreak of mad cow disease starting in 1996 in Great Britain and spreading to Europe greatly affected the meat supply there. International quarantines were imposed on European cattle and meat, but the large supplies of meat from other countries averted any scarcity on the Continent. Crop failures in one country, especially among the developed countries, almost never result in severe shortages or suffering because of the global supply system. And in the poorer regions such as sub-Saharan Africa, where starvation is not uncommon, speedy relief efforts by governments and humanitarian organizations manage to alleviate hardship unless political strongmen or corrupt officials interfere.

Adjusting and realigning trade policies on agriculture have another dimension. In the United States the "agrarian myth"—the fondness and admiration for the rural way of life—enables agricultural interests to obtain strong support systems, which in turn affects international trade. In Japan, farmers also enjoy a certain reverence, and Europeans have a strong sense of compassion for the family farm. These deeply rooted cultural attitudes justify governmental programs supporting farmers, which become important during trade negotiations. The United States wants to penetrate overseas agricultural markets for the sake of export trade, but it encounters resistance. By the same token, as it strives to remove barriers to its own markets, it maintains some restrictions on the domestic market due to political sensitivity.

Because of the importance of the export market, agricultural interests lobby for and support trade agreements. In fact, agriculture has generally been the strongest proponent of trade liberalization, often generating some of America's trade agreements, and no industry had a more global outlook and perspective than cotton. It originated the idea for the P.L. 480 program as a device to increase overseas sales, and it started other promotional programs in conjunction with the U.S. Department of Agriculture such as the Cotton Council International.

Agriculture has profited from NAFTA, which went into effect in 1994. Corn producers were the greatest beneficiaries, with the export value of corn rising from $340,440,000 in 1994 to $1,002,717,000 in 1996. A similar, though not so large, improvement occurred with wheat, cotton, and rice. The losers were poultry and beef cattle. Poultry fell from $213,597,000 in 1994 to $202,053,000 in 1996, and a corresponding blow hit the cattle industry: from $98,895,000 to $56,052,000 during the same period. Tariffs today remain on some farm products, but all tariffs will be phased out over a period ranging from five to fifteen years. Only a few items remain on the fifteen-year phase-out list: orange juice, melons, peanuts, sugar, and certain fresh vegetables.[7]

A new partner in world trade may, however, bring serious competition to American farmers. Agricultural interests have always longed to penetrate the China market, and the latter's membership in the WTO is expected to make that goal possible. The cotton industry began to feel the effect of China's competition on the world market by the mid-1990s, even though the country was not yet a member of the WTO. By 2002 producers of other commodities saw that China would be a tough competitor once it joined the WTO. China purchased a large share of U.S. agricultural exports in 2000, but it could easily buy less from American producers and it could also become a major exporter to Japan and undercut U.S. sales there. Historically, farm interests supported free trade, but the fear of China brought them a new degree of caution.[8] Globalization and technology are changing the traditional structure of world agriculture, even though food production has risen and prices have fallen despite the increase in world population. Small farms, particularly in the United States, are declining, and the structure of the world's system of agribusiness continues to undergo transition.

Technology accounts for much of the change. Within the United States, mechanization greatly reduced the numbers of farm workers, but along with new developments in pesticides and herbicides and new cultivation practices, it also significantly increased crop yields. A similar, though reduced, effect occurred around the world, amplifying the food supply while reducing the rural population, but enabling developing countries to engage in global agricultural trade. Farmers and commodity brokers have begun to rely on information technology, too. Advances in agriculture include global positioning systems, which allow a landowner to adjust irrigation and fertilizer on a per-acre basis. With other devices, grain harvesters can measure the yield per acre. Such advances make farming a high-tech industry requiring greater capitalization and even more dependence on the global market.

The rise of biotechnology in agriculture brought more changes to the industry. Research scientists have developed insect-resistant Bt crops or transgenic plants. This advance showed promise for increasing yields, a particularly important factor in poorer countries, and for reducing the use of pesticides in fighting harmful insects. Hoping to cash in on the new technology, companies such as DuPont and Aventis purchased traditional seed companies such as Delta Pine and Land. They hoped to develop the new varieties of Bt crops. As discussed further in Chapter 6, Aventis, a French company, developed StarLink corn and made it available to farmers in the United States and elsewhere. In 2000, however, Friends of the Earth, an environmental organization, discovered that Bt proteins were found in several corn products commonly available on grocery shelves. Because Bt crops were thought to be harmful to monarch butterflies and might cause allergies in humans, this discovery—though unproven—set off an uproar. When StarLink corn was taken off the market, many farmers were left with large stores.

StarLink became a global issue because it caused a loss of export sales and sparked the fear that foreign-grown crops could contaminate the U.S. food supply. In view of the global trade in agriculture, the issue had the potential to damage severely U.S. export sales and raised issues of public health. The United Nations Human Development Program reported that opposition to the further development of transgenic crops could endanger the efforts by poorer countries to feed their people. Wealthy countries with ample food supplies worried about Bt effects on health, while poorer countries saw Bt crops as a possible answer to food shortages. This sharp contrast illustrated the concerns that grew out of the globalization of agriculture.[9]

The growth of international tourism furnishes another excellent example of the development of globalization since 1945. It combines the forces of technology and economic development with the rise of mass consumerism in a fashion that is unique to the latter twentieth century. According to one claim, "By 1992 [tourism] had become the largest industry and largest employer in the world."[10] From an economic and cultural perspective, tourism should be understood as a major factor in the growth of the world-integrated economy.

A set of circumstances was responsible for this development. To begin with, the higher standard of living in the developed countries provided the expanding middle class with the funds and leisure time to take vacations. The spread of unionization, which made annual vacations a worker's right, spurred the growth of tourism, too. Union influence and the robust economy, particularly among the Western nations, enabled large corporations to establish pension funds for their employees. Along with pension benefits came health insurance or government-sponsored health coverage for many wage earners, another innovation in the postwar era. Social Security, which went into operation in 1935, served as the foundation for retirees' income in the United States. For the first time in the country's history, both salaried and hourly wage earners accrued a sound retirement pension via private and public channels, and retirees became a rising new subgroup with disposable income as early as the 1970s. Improved public education and exposure through television heightened people's geographic knowledge and cultural awareness. Not to be overlooked was the immunization of tourists from various diseases through public and private health sources that made international travel less risky. For good reason, one writer stated that "travel and tourism have become an institutionalized way of life for most of the world's middle class."[11]

Until the advent of jet aircraft in the late 1950s and early 1960s, international travel remained largely a luxury of the upper classes.

Cross-border or transoceanic travel was slow, often by ship, and required more time and money than middle-class income earners could afford. Americans going overseas preferred Western Europe, generally choosing England and France as their destinations. War-torn countries and those in the Soviet bloc were, of course, not popular sites. Traditional attractions such as classical ruins, famous buildings and landmarks, and resort areas grabbed the bulk of American tourists. As it became evident that tourists provided a source of revenue, government agencies at all levels began to market and exploit their assets through advertising. The reconstruction of the European economy, supplemented by American aid, helped to restore the cachet of vacationing in Europe.

Certainly the most important factor in making tourism the world's largest service industry was the development of commercial jet aircraft. In 1949 propeller craft took about eighteen hours to reach London from New York, traveling at 250–300 miles per hour. By 1969, when jet planes became readily available, the same trip took only seven hours. By 1990, the time remained roughly the same, but the cost had declined to about 3–4 cents per mile compared with 31 cents in 1949 and 8 cents in 1979. The improved comforts of air travel and greater ease in making reservations, which by 2002 could be handled on personal computers, brought a boom in international travel. In this case, technology served as the main force in promoting globalization. One commentator was prompted to write: "In the post war period the airplane has acted as the most dynamic element in the world passenger traffic, increasing its share significantly to dominate the public transportation in North America."[12]

Technology as seen in aircraft obviously contributed to the growth of tourism, but changes in lifestyle as basic as the perception of the pursuit of happiness were important. Americans' puritanical attitude toward work and leisure had begun to change prior to World War II, and it underwent a significant alteration afterward. Recreation came to be regarded as a human right. Indeed, in 1948 the United Nations stated in its Universal Declaration of Human Rights that "everyone has the right to rest and leisure, including reasonable limitation of working hours and periodic holidays with pay."[13] As unionization spread in the industrialized countries, vacations became more common, so that a combination of increased leisure time and affordable fares on jet aircraft gave an unprecedented boost to tourism. The greater productivity of the U.S. economy during the same years also contributed to the growth of service industries, with tourism being the greatest beneficiary. "The more time we save in making goods," wrote one observer, "the more time we spend for services."[14] This phenomenon of increased leisure time and shorter hours of work became more apparent starting in the 1970s, owing to the impact of computer technology on productivity as well as the greater number of educated people in the United States. Knowledge bred curiosity and the desire to travel.

Again, transnational or multinational corporations took the lead in the globalization of tourism. Airlines, hotel chains, restaurants, recreational companies such as Disney, and rental car agencies took advantage of the new technologies and paved the way for the vacation traveler. Whether visitors to Greek and Roman ruins or fun-seekers at Disney World, tourists had reliable transportation, housing, and food. Even though cultural purists denounced the standardization and crass consumerism of commercial tourism, currency-laden travelers left behind the cash sorely needed by the host countries, particularly in the developing countries, which regarded tourist spending as a source of funds to stimulate trade and currency exchanges.

International tourism grew. By 1960, arrivals into foreign lands were 600 percent higher than in 1950, and when 425 million international tourists were counted in 1990, the total represented a sixteenfold increase over 1950.[15] During these four decades, Europe ranked as the most popular destination and North America as the second. Toward the end of the twentieth century, Asia became a significant attraction, owing in great part to the new prosperity of Japan that sent tourists to China, Hong Kong, South Korea, and Singapore. Africa, the Middle East, and South Asia drew the fewest tourists because of their lack of infrastructure and marketing. Political instability also kept tourists out of some areas.

Tourism reinforced the power of transnationals. Governments saw that they needed tourists to generate jobs and earn dollars for currency exchange, making them dependent on hotel chains and commercial airlines. The multinational corporations involved in the tourist business quickly learned to negotiate directly with these governments in order to obtain property rights and establish "safety zones" for travelers. With the economic power and business skills to make an area attractive to tourists, the transnational corporations were able to make demands and win concessions. Sometimes the result was a mixed blessing for the host country: cash flowed from tourists, but a portion of control was lost to the corporations. Local residents often complained about the commercialization of their homeland and the influx of cultural behavior and practices that violated their own values.

So great are the benefits, however, that developing countries generally regard the transnationals as an asset. Tourist spending has a far-reaching effect: it stimulates household incomes, provides tax revenues, encourages business investment, and attracts still more commercial activities. The construction industry nearly always experiences a boom, if only temporarily, and other secondary beneficiaries include transportation, small manufacturing, and energy providers. Multinationals involved in the tourist trade consequently enjoy much respect and support around the world, even though the locals may resent their intrusion.

Tourism truly became a global business, as evidenced by the efforts by international organizations to promote it. The World Bank regularly supported efforts in developing countries for commercial tourism, as in the case of Latin America, where several nations sought to replicate Spain's success in becoming a major tourist attraction.[16] During the 1970s the Dominican Republic created INFRATUR, an organization that sought to build a special area for tourists, known as the Playa Dorado and Playa Grande, and that obtained funds from the World Bank. With this stimulus, the economy jumped; hotel investments increased and tourism grew. By the latter 1980s, 1.4 million visitors were traveling to the Dominican Republic.[17]

As the world recovered from World War II and vacations became a regular feature of life, at least in the industrial countries, tourism thus received recognition as a dynamic and creative economic force. In 1970 members of the International Union for Official Tourism Organizations (IUOTO) formed the World Tourism Organization (WTO). Headquartered in Madrid, it became affiliated with the United Nations in 1976 as an executing agency. By 1997, it had over 100 nation members and worked closely with governments and private enterprise. Like any trade group, the WTO—not to be confused with the World Trade Organization—gathers statistics and marketing data, improves communications among commercial tourist agencies, and disseminates information. Its primary focus is development.

Crisis management has become an important new area of responsibility for the WTO. The 2001 terrorist attack on the World Trade Center in New York City upset the normal flow of tourists, with a dramatic economic impact. The travel industry suffered immeasurably as vacationers and travelers postponed or cancelled trips out of fear of terrorism. At its annual meeting in Osaka, Japan, in October 2001, the WTO condemned terrorism, with Secretary-General Francesco Frangialli stating that "terrorism is the direct enemy of tourism."[18] For the next year, tourism was expected to fall by 50 percent, prompting the WTO to call for cooperation in eradicating terrorism. These actions and other efforts by governments to establish a viable tourist trade demonstrate the emergence of tourism as a critical force in the global economy.

Serious concerns have arisen over the impact of tourism. Its effects on local residents and on the environment are the most important. Vacationers expect comfort and conveniences and often have preconceived notions of native culture. "The tourist enclaves that are created," wrote a travel specialist, "thus have more to do with tourists' fantasies than with the culture of the host country."[19] The social structure in some cases becomes more rigid in host countries because the upper and middle classes benefit while the lower classes, who are relegated to menial jobs, fall in stature. Damage to local habitats occur as tourists literally traipse over fragile flora and historic sites.

Also among the top industries involved in the new global economy are textiles. The staples necessary for life—food, shelter, and clothing—explain the importance of textiles in the world economy. The relative strength of the industry, which combines fabric and apparel, symbolizes the changing nature of the U.S. economy and demonstrates the interrelationship of the forces affecting American manufactures: global competition, currency values, and the role of government. New technologies also have an impact on price and the ability of mill owners to compete in the world market. And because aspiring Third World countries depend on textiles for economic development, the industry generally stands at the forefront of trade disputes and policy changes. It is a major employer in some areas of the United States such as the Southeast and the rural southern Cotton Belt. Textiles and apparel together account for about 10 percent of the jobs in the U.S. economy. They affect people in agriculture who produce cotton and wool; mill workers engaged in the spinning and processing of fibers and fabrics, both natural and synthetic; designers and garment workers in the apparel business; and eventually retailers in the clothing industry. A large number of countries manufacture textiles for export, which explains why some of the most complex trade arrangements in the world's integrated economy involve this particular industry. In fact, the United States provided considerable protection from foreign competition in textiles despite its belief in free trade.[20]

Until the late 1950s, American textile and apparel manufacturers enjoyed a strong domestic and international market. There were, for example, about 1.3 million textile workers in 1945 and another 2 million in the apparel industry. Consumer demand grew steadily in the postwar decade. Thanks to the efforts by the United States to rebuild the war-torn economies of Europe and Asia, the export trade was strong and the industry was prosperous. In this respect, textiles reflected the general condition of the American economy.

Japan was the first to emerge as a competitor. The United States encouraged the rebuilding of textile mills there as part of its plan to restore its market for cotton that had been lost during World War II. By the mid-1950s, the British, one of the leading textile producers, complained about the intrusion of Japanese exports into the world market. Japan used the income derived from textiles to capitalize other industries, a practice noticed by developing countries. "Japan was a role model," according to one author, that "many developing countries attempted to emulate."[21] Other nations such as Pakistan and India also exported fabrics. This competition became a threat to American companies starting in the late 1950s, which prompted Washington to modify its trade policies on textiles.

Japan now posed a danger. It clearly had the potential to seize a large share of the U.S. market with low-wage imports. Flexing their political muscle, the textile companies managed to get exceptions to GATT, known as "voluntary export restraints" (VER), which enabled the United States to reduce Japanese imports. Europe's developed countries used a similar plan to get Japan to reduce its exports voluntarily. Low-wage imports continued, nonetheless, to enter the United States until the 1970s, when the issue acquired strong political support.

That decade proved critical in world trade for more industries than only textiles. For one thing, the United States went off the fixed gold exchange and let the American dollar float. In 1973 the Organization of Petroleum Exporting Countries (OPEC) imposed the oil embargo that set off a wave of inflation in the industrial world. The end of the Bretton Woods system also contributed. Markets for U.S. textile exports in the industrialized countries declined, while developing countries used the abundant supply of OPEC's petrodollars to initiate textile processing and manufacturing. For the American textile industry, this change brought growth in imports of manufactured clothing and other finished goods, known as "end products"—a disturbing trend for the industry.

A critical factor in the policy for textiles and apparel dealt with synthetics. Prior to the 1970s, U.S. restrictions on imports applied only to cotton fabrics. Developing countries concentrated on producing synthetic fabrics and skirted around the U.S. restrictions, thus eroding the market for cotton. For this reason, American fashion relied heavily on polyester and other synthetics during the 1970s. American textile firms sustained a considerable loss of the world's market share and felt the intrusion of foreign competition. Low-wage labor enabled the developing countries to compete effectively in the U.S. market. As was the case with agriculture, the relative ease poorer countries had in starting their own textile and apparel industries caused the American manufacturers to be among one of the first industries to experience global competition.

American textile manufacturers used this argument to justify their demands for protection, and the fact that so many jobs depended on the textile mills and apparel companies gave the industry political clout. In trying to accommodate the needs of a major industry with a large number of workers, the federal government managed to get a major exception made to GATT, the free-trade organization that it strongly supported. The first of a series of 1973 agreements among GATT members regarding textiles and apparel became operative in 1974: the Multi-Fiber Agreement (MFA). It deviated from the free-trade spirit of GATT and encountered harsh criticism, but the pressing demands imposed on governments in the United States and Europe from textile interests forced them into it.

In essence, the MFA permitted bilateral agreements (involving two countries only) that enabled countries to "manage" their trade in textiles and apparel. GATT allowed developed countries such as the United States to impose import controls through the use of quotas, or limits on imports, on a renewable basis. MFA negotiators periodically revised their rules with complex formulas involving price differentials, "burden sharing," rules of origin, and countervailing duties.[22] No aspect of international trade had such complex regulations as textiles and apparel. Despite this effort, low-wage imports continued to penetrate the U.S. market. The inability of the MFA to provide the protection the industry wanted, together with the criticism of the agreement from developing countries, particularly as the United States continued to promote free trade, were the principal factors in the drive to replace GATT with the World Trade Organization.

Under the new organization, restrictions on textiles would be phased out over a ten-year period. Until that point, quotas might be imposed, but not on a renewable basis. Tariffs could be reduced. An importing country might slap a three-year restraint on goods from a particular country if it felt threatened. For the proponents of trade agreements, these restrictions were necessary during the decade of phasing out the heavy and complex restrictions dating back to the late 1950s. Countries that were not members of the World Trade Organization would still face tariffs and other restrictions.

Another major agreement that affected the industry in the latter 1990s was NAFTA. During the intense political battle over its ratification, the U.S. textile mills and apparel companies strongly supported it. They saw a chance to enter the Mexican market, anticipating as much as a 25 percent increase in total sales. Restrictions on imports from Mexico prior to ratification would be phased out over a ten-year period. In 2002 the process of implementing NAFTA continued, but it had encountered little resistance from the industry, although the textile unions strongly resented it.

Textiles and apparel have occupied a central and key position in the development of the world's integrated economy since World War II. At first, textile manufacturers encouraged unrestricted trade and had little objection to the American efforts to rebuild the industry in countries devastated by the war. Their position changed, however, as Japan and developing countries relied on textile exports to improve their own economies and penetrated the American market. In fighting for protection, the United States had to move back from its stance on free trade. Other industries such as steel had a similar experience, and the success of the United States in facing and meeting its competitors in the global economy remained to be seen.

From the perspective of the consumer, however the automobile industry best illustrates the globalization of the U.S. economy. No industry or product better exemplified the nation's pride and strength. It stood as a mighty symbol of innovation and ingenuity from the standpoints both of industrial progress and social mobility. Americans indeed saw their automobiles as manifestations of the "American dream" of prosperity and success.

In 1945 the pent-up demand for consumer goods placed great emphasis on automobile ownership. People were tired of the economic deprivations of the Great Depression and the sacrifices imposed by World War II, and they eagerly sought a more comfortable lifestyle. Automobiles ranked high on their list, second only to home ownership, and the savings accumulated by workers during the war could now be spent. With gasoline and steel no longer diverted to the war effort, automobile production and use soared steadily throughout the postwar period. The popularity of American automobiles kept out foreign competition, and the "Big Three" manufacturers—Chrysler, Ford, and General Motors—dominated the domestic market.

As was the case with other industries, automobiles went through a period of severe adjustment in the 1970s. In this case, the oil embargo of 1973 that followed soaring oil prices set by OPEC clearly served as the cause. Although inroads into the American market had been made by foreign manufacturers, noticeably Volkswagen, it was not until the embargo that consumers demanded more fuel-efficient automobiles. The Big Three had overlooked the importance of fuel economy and thereby opened the door to global competition. Japanese makers such as Toyota and Datsun, a subsidiary of Nissan, had already established a small market base, but with the embargo and especially the entry of Honda into the United States, American auto companies quickly felt the erosion of their oligopoly. "While huge, gas-guzzling land vessels lumbered off American assembly lines," wrote one observer, "the Japanese cranked out small, nimble cars with relatively petite fuel appetites."[23] Quality figured into consumer choice as the snappy smaller cars from Japan quickly engendered customer loyalty due to their reliability. Neighborhood car dealers now featured overseas models along with the traditional American cars. So great was the invasion from Japan that Chrysler's sales dipped until the company teetered on the brink of extinction. Only with a bailout in 1980, a government guarantee of a $2 billion loan, did Chrysler overcome the threat of bankruptcy. The industry lost its predominance. According to one trade analyst, "Indeed, the car has become the symbol of American manufacturing decline."[24]

The average citizen easily grasped the global ramifications. Seeing the proliferation of small, foreign automobiles on the streets and roads of America provided indisputable evidence that the economy was becoming interconnected with countries around the world.

Resistance to the competition came from the automakers and their supporters, particularly the United Automobile Workers.

Like textiles, the automobile industry pressured the White House and Congress to place restrictions on Japanese imports. These came in the form of "voluntary export restraints," the same tactic employed on behalf of the textile industry. Initiated through the White House in 1981, the VER constituted an agreement by the Japanese to restrict their automobile exports to the United States by limiting the number to 1.6 million cars for two years; the quota was raised to 1.8 million through 1985, and by 1993 the figure stood at 2.3 million per year. In order to overcome these restrictions, Japanese manufacturers opened assembly plants in the United States, in effect making the U.S. auto industry even more global. Honda opened its first plant in Ohio in 1982, and other companies such as Toyota, Nissan, Mazda, and Mitsubishi followed.[25]

American automobile companies had extended their own operations internationally prior to the onslaught of foreign competition. Ford Motor Company spread into Canada in 1905 with a plant at Windsor, Ontario, and General Motors acquired a Canadian carmaker in 1918. Moreover, both companies had penetrated markets in Europe and Latin America prior to World War II. In 1967, Ford restructured its operations in Europe into one organization, Ford Europe. It intended to achieve greater efficiency and lower costs of production and in the 1970s came out with the Ford Fiesta for the European market.[26] Still facing stiff competition, the company reorganized again and combined the American and European divisions into Ford Automotive Operations. General Motors expanded and rearranged its European operations but maintained a different corporate structure than Ford. Both had little success with the Asian market, which continued to be dominated by the Japanese and the emerging South Korean car manufacturers.

Hoping to boost exports, Washington initiated discussions with Tokyo in 1993 that enabled manufacturers to gain better access to their markets. This National Export Strategy improved exports by 22 percent during 1992–1995. Sales by U.S. carmakers to Japan increased the most, jumping by 250 percent. The inauguration of NAFTA also helped exports, with sales increasing by 250 percent during the first year of the agreement. Because of a Mexican recession, sales declined the next year, but not below the pre-NAFTA level. During the 1992–1995 period, a 42 percent increase in sales to Korea occurred. These statistics reflect greater U.S. sales in the world market, but they do not indicate the extent of automobiles' status as a globalized industry.[27]

The number of foreign cars made in the United States rose steadily as did imports from Europe and Asia. In 2000 imports accounted for 22.8 percent of the total U.S. market in passenger cars, but Japanese manufacturers with factories in the United States, even though they produced domestically, pushed the total of foreign models to 45 percent. For light trucks, which include sport utility vehicles (SUVs), the United States fared much better than the competition, producing 77.2 percent of domestic sales compared with only 55 percent in passenger cars. European makers accounted for 13.2 percent of the passenger car imports in 2000, with Volkswagen and Mercedes-Benz registering the largest increase.[28]

Along with vehicle sales came a global network of manufacturers and suppliers of replacement parts and accessories. Ford and General Motors built parts factories in Canada, Europe, and Mexico and also made supply arrangements with foreign manufacturers. The largest U.S. parts companies in Europe had sales of over $1 billion. As reported by Standard & Poor's, the United States has nonetheless had a trade deficit in auto parts since 1983. Domestic automobile companies had few parts-manufacturing plants in Japan, which accounted for a large portion of the trade deficit.

Information technology facilitated the expansive international trade in automobiles and parts. As might be expected, large and small firms relied on the Internet and computer-generated communications for their daily business transactions. Competition came not only from local suppliers but also from areas around the world. The growth of this industry on an international basis intensified capital flows.

World competition improved the quality and fuel efficiency of American automobiles and gave consumers a wider range of models to choose from. Because of consumer taste, the U.S. trade deficit in automobiles and parts widened, however, as much as 72 percent during 1995–1999. Expressed in dollars, the deficit reached $103 billion in 1999. Exports of U.S. vehicles rose 17 percent, but imports jumped 44 percent during the same period. Even though the automobile industry has become a global giant, with its leading companies qualifying as transnational corporations, it has remained a highly competitive industry dependent on consumer preference. No industry exemplified the characteristics and operations of transnationals and their role in the world-integrated economy better than automobiles.

A review of several major industries in the United States demonstrates that globalization began to move forward soon after World War II. In the case of agriculture, it began with the desire to restore the trade lost during the previous generations, but with the others, particularly tourism, it was owing to the reconstructed economies of Europe and Asia plus social and economic improvements in the developed countries. The rise of leisure time, labor rights, technological improvements in transportation, public health advances—indeed, a host of worldwide developments in the last half-century—brought about the globalization of many industries. Transnationals obviously were essential in the growth of international markets and commerce, but they relied on the various technologies and trade agreements developed over the past fifty years.

An examination of these major industries reveals the early initiatives taken by the United States upon the close of World War II to restore its foreign markets. Until the 1970s, American corporate giants faced minor competition, but a series of events as sweeping as the OPEC embargo set in motion new developments that placed the country's economy in a more competitive environment. Through trade negotiations, American transnationals fought back by gaining better access to competitors' markets and by taking advantage of new international agreements. In the words of one economist, the United States has become "increasingly integrated into the economic activities of foreign countries."[29]

NOTES

1. Richard J. Barnet and Ronald E. Muller, *Global Reach: The Power of the Multinational Corporations* (New York: Simon and Schuster, 1974), 35–36.
2. Ibid., 14.
3. Melvin E. Sims, "U.S. Marketing Practices around the World," in U.S. Department of Agriculture, *U.S. Agriculture in a Global Economy: 1985 Yearbook of Agriculture* (Washington, DC, 1985), 347–48.
4. *The Economist* (March 25, 2000): 9.
5. Ibid.
6. D. Clayton Brown, "The International Institute for Cotton: The Globalization of Cotton since 1945," *Agricultural History* 74 (Spring 2000): 258–71.
7. NAFTA Impact on Agriculture, http://www.ers.usda.gov/briefing/NAFTA/impact.htm, 2002.
8. *Loveland (Colorado) Daily Report-Herald*, August 11, 2001.
9. *Progressive Farmer* (September 2001): 64.
10. Theobald, *Global Tourism*, 1.

11. Ibid., 4.
12. Zbigniew Mieczkowski, *World Trends in Tourism and Recreation* (New York: Peter Lang, 1990), 124.
13. Ibid., 83.
14. Quote appears in ibid., 85.
15. David Harrison, ed., *Tourism and the Less Developed Countries* (New York: Halsted Press, 1992), 3.
16. Regina G. Schluter, "Tourism Development: A Latin American Perspective," in *Global Tourism*, 247–48; Emanuel de Kadt, *Tourism: Passport to Development? Perspectives on the Social and Cultural Effects of Tourism in Developing Countries* (New York: Oxford University Press, 1979), v.
17. Schluter, "Tourism Development," 249.
18. General Assembly Unifies Global Tourism Industry in Crisis, http://www.world-tourism.org/newsroom/Releases/more_releases/gadaily06.htm, 2002.
19. De Kadt, *Tourism: Passport to Development?*, 13.
20. Kitty G. Dickerson, *Textiles and Apparel in the Global Economy*, 3d ed. (Upper Saddle River, NJ: Merrill, 1999), 138–66.
21. Kitty G. Dickerson, *Textiles and Apparel in the Global Economy*, 2d ed. (Englewood Cliffs, NJ: Prentice-Hall, 1995), 128.
22. Ibid., 340–41.
23. Philip A. Mundo, *National Politics in a Global Economy: The Domestic Sources of U.S. Trade Policy* (Washington, DC: Georgetown University Press, 1999), 245.
24. Ibid.
25. Dicken, *Global Shift*, 339.
26. Ibid., 343–44.
27. Joseph C. Tardiff, ed., *U.S. Industry Profiles: The Leading 100* (Detroit: Gale, 1998), 398–99.
28. Standard & Poor's, *Industry Surveys: Autos and Auto Parts* (New York: McGraw-Hill, June 14, 2001), 7.
29. Carbaugh, *International Economics*, 3.

5 Immigration

Immigration and globalization reinforce one another. The migration of people into a country, or their emigration out, exerts a strong influence on nearly every aspect of a society: the economy, social and cultural life, politics, and even demographics. No country owes more to immigration than the United States. From its colonial period through the end of the twentieth century, it has served as a beacon to people around the world who seek a new life. For no small reason does Liberty raise her torch in New York Harbor and beckon:

> Give me your tired, your poor,
> Your huddled masses yearning to breathe free,
> The wretched refuse of your teeming shore,
> Send these, the homeless, tempest-tossed, to me:
> I lift my lamp beside the golden door.

These words of Emma Lazarus acknowledged the courage and aspirations of millions of new arrivals to the United States long before the Statue of Liberty was erected in 1886. Now, at the start of the millennium, immigration and globalization go together, as seen in a statement from a recent study: "It is impossible to separate the globalization of trade and capital from the global movement of people."[1]

In the pursuit of free trade after 1945, as the United States tried to remove barriers to international commerce, migration across its borders became easier. A more relaxed immigration policy and a strong domestic economy brought a new influx of people starting in the 1970s. During the eighteen-year period of 1981–1998, the number of immigrants reached an astounding 14,943,000, but this total did not include illegal entrants. Statistics on the illegal resident population can only be estimated, but the Immigration and Naturalization Service (INS) put the number at 5 million in 1996. The second-highest rate of newcomers on a historical basis came during 1901–1920.

The rate of arrivals after 1980, particularly in regard to illegals, became a matter of controversy. Globalists tended to favor the influx of workers and usually focused on the economic dimensions of immigration, but some went further and insisted that immigration was the nation's lifeblood. G. Pascal Zachary, the author of *Global Me*, asserted that "countries must diversify their ethnic, racial and national character or face economic, demographic and social stagnation."[2] By contrast, presidential candidate Pat Buchanan wrote: "Uncontrolled immigration threatens to deconstruct the nation we grew up in and convert America into a conglomeration of peoples with almost nothing in common—not history, heroes, language, culture, faith, or ancestors."[3]

Historical perspective must be considered when examining the role of immigration in the globalization of the United States. In 1819, Congress passed legislation requiring that immigrants be counted. Congress placed no restrictions, however, on entering the country; those persons arriving in the United States were free to stay. Most of the newcomers came from northern Europe, but Asians also came to the United States to work in railroad construction or to seek their fortunes in the gold rush. As the number of Chinese laborers soared, Congress passed the Chinese Exclusion Act in 1882. Starting in the 1880s, the preponderance of arrivals then came from southern and eastern Europe. During the years shortly before the outbreak of World War I, 1900–1914, about 1 million "New Immigrants" came each year. This wave of people into the United States produced expressions of concern and even resentment and hostility toward immigrants. A series of restrictions went into effect that climaxed with the Immigration Act of 1924, which ended the open access to America's shores.

Immigration dropped but did not stop. The new measure imposed a quota that gave preferential treatment to Europeans from Britain, Germany, and Scandinavia. No Asians were permitted except for Filipinos, who had status as American nationals because the Philippines became a U.S. territory following the Spanish-American War. Immigration had now become selective, and once the Great Depression of the 1930s hit, the flow was "reduced to a trickle" of about 50,000 per year, according to one historian.[4] During the 1940s an increase occurred owing to refugees fleeing the horrors of World War II and to postwar humanitarianism. The McCarran-Walter Act of 1952 gave preference to relatives of U.S. citizens and to spouses and children of resident aliens. For the 1950s immigration rose again, but not dramatically, reaching a total of 2.5 million.

Because the 1924 act exempted countries in the Western Hemisphere, Canadians came in sizeable numbers during the 1950s–1970s: 9,475,000. These "next-door neighbors" aroused no concern or hostility because they spoke English and were familiar with American customs. Such immigrants, like those from the British Isles, seemed "invisible" and nonthreatening. For the rest of the century after 1970, at least through 1998, Canadian immigration dropped to 2,317,000.

Mexican immigration, thanks also to the 1924 act, has a special place in U.S. history. A large area of the Southwest and West Coast belonged to Mexico until it became U.S. territory with the Mexican War of 1846. The creation of a national boundary through their homeland did not cut off Mexicans from family and relatives south of the border. They began the practice of cross-border migration, coming into the United States and returning home. In order to supply temporary labor for agriculture during the wartime manpower shortage, the Roosevelt administration instituted the Bracero Program for Mexican laborers in 1942 that continued until 1965. Some 450,000 *braceros* (laborers) entered the country in 1959 alone. Many of them remained, however, illegally. Aside from *braceros* and other illegals, about 300,000 Mexicans emigrated into the United States in the 1950s.

Asians faced severe restrictions. Although Chinese were excluded in 1882, a small number of Japanese and Koreans were admitted and settled mostly on the West Coast. Under special circumstances a limited number of Chinese, Japanese, and Koreans could enter the country if they had a sponsor such as a business. In 1917, Asian Indians were excluded. This movement for restriction reached its peak with the Immigration Act of 1924, which, as noted, closed the door to Japanese and Koreans as well. Moreover, federal law forbade Asians from becoming naturalized citizens. The reasons for the exclusionary policy toward Asians stemmed from fear of competition for jobs, concern that too many Asians would overwhelm American culture, and racism. Asians immigrating to the United States had to contend with discrimination and second-class status.

Changes began to occur during World War II. In 1943 the United States repealed its exclusions on Chinese entrants because China was an ally in the war against Japan. Further liberalization came with the

War Brides Act of 1945, which allowed foreign wives of American soldiers into the United States, and the Refugee Act of 1953, which enabled Koreans to enter the country in the aftermath of the Korean War. Like immigrants of nearly all nationalities, Asians benefited from the 1952 McCarran-Walter Act, which permitted relatives and spouses to enter the country without regard for the quota imposed in 1924.

From the perspective of the postmodern period of American immigration—the years since 1965—these earlier restrictions were significant. The exclusionist policies meant that the United States had a small Asian population concentrated on the West Coast. Asians generally tended to live together in their ethnic neighborhoods, and since many of them were male, they often resided in labor camps. Although they clearly cannot be regarded as "invisible," a large percentage of them had menial jobs and exerted little political or economic influence. In other words, Asian immigration had a negligible impact.

Prior to 1924, immigration into the United States was generally open and free of qualifications. There were few restrictions until the latter nineteenth century, when the government targeted Asians because of the resentment toward them on the West Coast. Viewed through the window of 1924–1965, immigrating into the country became, however, more difficult and selective. This restrictive period occurred during the Great Depression and coincided with World War II. A large number of immigrants during this period seemed "invisible," coming from English-speaking nations and blending easily into American society. For nearly the half-century prior to 1965, immigration had thus slowed, posing no threat to wage scales or to the ethnic demography of the United States because the quota system, established in 1924, allowed Europeans to dominate. Only the cross-border migration of Mexicans provided an exception to these circumstances, but these people had long been resident in the Southwest, and although they suffered from discrimination, their presence provoked little demand for restriction. In 1965 these conditions began to change, and a new history of immigration started to unfold that accelerated the ethnic diversity of the United States, thereby broadening its global outlook.

When Congress passed the Immigration Act of 1965, it removed the quota system and liberalized further the provisions for relatives and spouses of citizens and resident aliens. Congress also equalized the number of immigrants from each hemisphere. As a consequence, immigrants during the last quarter-century entered the country in unprecedented numbers, so much so that some writers referred to this development as the "Second Great Migration," or second "wave," after the huge influx of New Immigrants about a century ago.

Latinos, particularly Mexicans, accounted for the largest percentage, but a notable increase also occurred with Asians. For the period 1981–1998, Mexicans entering legally reached 3,586,000, more than the entire total from 1820 to 1979. Latin American countries that traditionally had not sent significant numbers now had a sizable increase: El Salvador, Haiti, Jamaica, the Dominican Republic, and Colombia. For the 1981–1998 period, these five countries alone had a total of 1,831,800 emigrants to the United States. Cuban immigration, which had jumped during the 1960s and 1970s, began tapering off after 1980. This astounding surge of humanity spread across America but concentrated in the Sunbelt. By the mid-1990s its demographic impact became most apparent in California and Texas.

A variety of factors accounted for the flow, often described as the "push" effect, meaning that depressed conditions in the migrants' homelands drove them to seek opportunity elsewhere. Mexico faced extreme pressure to furnish employment for its people because its economy depended overwhelmingly on agriculture until about 1960, when industrialization and services began to expand. Surplus farm workers went into the growth sectors by about 50 percent by the mid-1990s, but this percentage was not enough. Population growth intensified the pressure, and adult workers had young families depending on them. High inflation, high production costs for industry, slow growth in the agricultural sector, and income disparities between the agricultural and industrial workers contributed to the social and economic stratification of the country. Extreme poverty among the rural inhabitants and urban disadvantaged became both a cause and an effect of the weak economy. By the last decade of the twentieth century, these conditions grew more severe. When in 1995 the country went through a financial crisis, alleviated only by a $52 billion loan from the United States, the Mexican government had to institute economic reforms.

Mexicans saw the United States as the only solution to their need for employment. Cross-border migration was characterized by legal migrants coming to establish themselves and become citizens and by illegal workers seeking to earn money and then return home. To an extent the United States served as a vent for the social and economic difficulties of Mexico. Unrest in the Chiapas region of southern Mexico, where the indigenous population rebelled against the government in 1994, resulted largely, though not entirely, from economic hardship.

In 1983, Jorge Bustamente, an authority on Mexican immigration, stated: "When undocumented workers go to the United States it does act as an economic safety valve for Mexico."[5]

Mexico was not alone among the Latin American countries suffering economic hardship. Similar conditions existed in Central America and parts of South America. In the 1960s the new Communist government of Fidel Castro drove Cuban refugees into the United States for both political and economic reasons. Political unrest and poverty spurred migrants to go to the United States from El Salvador, Guatemala, the Dominican Republic, and Puerto Rico. Mexico accounted for the largest number, of course, because of its immediate proximity to the United States. In the Mexican psyche, too, the American Southwest might be regarded as a second home.

A difficult but important aspect of U.S. immigration involved the large number of illegal migrants crossing the southern border. Again, Mexico accounted for most of them. A precise count of illegals is not possible, but the INS estimate in 1996 of 5 million does not appear incongruous. These people came for the same reasons as legal migrants, to seek employment and income, but many of them had no intention of staying. American farmers and ranchers had long depended on seasonal migratory labor, much of which consisted of illegal or undocumented workers. It was a common practice for the U.S. Border Patrol to relax its supervision during the harvest season when growers needed labor. Some migrants deliberately avoided the Bracero Program because it was more expedient to deal directly with employers. For many Mexicans, living and working in the United States on a seasonal basis had long been a regular feature of life. During the twenty years after World War II, the number of Latino illegal migrants—at least those apprehended by the INS—remained generally small, but a steady increase began in 1965 owing in part to the end of the Bracero Program. Latinos continued to cross the border illegally so that nine of the ten fastest-growing countries supplying undocumented immigrants by the mid-1990s were Latin American. The average annual growth for 1992–1996, less the number from Canada, was 267,000, with Latinos making up over 60 percent of the estimated illegal population in 1996.[6]

A parallel boost occurred with Asian immigrants, although the number of illegals was smaller. The 1924 legislation had kept the Asian population low in the United States. It was estimated at 900,000 in 1960, but the new act of 1965 opened the door so that by 1980 the population reached 3.5 million.[7] Vietnam, China, India, and the Philippines ranked among the top ten suppliers of Asian immigrants for 1981–1996. Of the total 13,484,275 immigrants during 1981–1996, Asians accounted for 2,600,556, according to the INS.[8]

Explanations for each sending country were varied because the socioeconomic conditions in Asia ranged from Japan's industrialized economy to severe pockets of poverty and distress extant throughout the continent. The political environment there included both socialist-oriented systems and economies geared to capitalism. Political and civil unrest characterized parts of the region, too, so that Asians seeking refuge from both instability and economic hardship looked to the United States as a haven. In the case of Vietnam, refugees from the Vietnam War, most of whom left their country after America's departure in 1975, gained entrance based on the Refugee Act of 1980. Asian Indian immigration had begun to increase in 1946 because of legislation making it easier for Indians to become naturalized U.S. citizens, but the influx during 1981–1996 amounted to almost 500,000.[9] Filipinos significantly increased in numbers after 1965, but in contrast to some other nationalities, a large percentage of them had business and technical skills that enabled them to assimilate easily into American life. Filipino women immigrants, many of whom were trained in health care, generally were better educated than men. In 1996 the INS estimated that nearly 100,000 Filipinos were living illegally in the United States.

In the case of Asian immigration, the less restrictive law of 1965 made the United States more accessible as a new homeland. In this respect, Asians resembled the Latinos who saw a chance for sharing the opportunities that America offered. Gone were the restrictions on Asian immigration, whether they stemmed from quotas or racism. For the United States, long the popular destination for emigrants around the world, the removal of restrictions brought a surge of Asians on a scale not seen since the nineteenth century. By 2000, the country had reached new heights of diversity and cultural pluralism.

The Immigration Act of 1965, a milestone in policy, could arguably have originated during World War II when the overwhelming refugee problem demanded a humanitarian response from the United States. Indeed, the evolving sense of openness toward the "huddled masses" paralleled the changing attitude toward civil rights. Another milestone in U.S. history, the Civil Rights Act of 1964 represented the culmination of a series of events and legislative measures that had

begun during World War II. Just as minorities enjoyed more acceptance after the mid-1960s, so did emigrants desiring to come to the
United States. They all benefited from America's greater emphasis on
and tolerance of diversity. As immigrants established new homes, particularly in the numbers of the last twenty-five years, they encouraged
diversity by virtue of their presence. Along with the poverty and other
hardships that "pushed" emigrants out of their native countries, the
new spirit of civil rights served to "pull" them to America. Hence, a
combination of circumstances, generally described as attitudes of social acceptance and the unsettling conditions in the postcolonial world,
blended together and set in motion the Second Great Migration.

Despite an easing of discrimination, sharp divisions arose over
the large influx of newcomers into the United States. Opposition to
immigration generally centered on economic issues such as loss of
jobs and lower wages. Some critics of globalization saw NAFTA as
responsible, claiming it opened Mexico to transnational corporations
that displaced rural people from their land or destroyed small businesses by building huge manufacturing plants and retail outlets. From
this vantage point, immigration was the consequence of ruthless competition waged by multinational corporations in developing countries,
which drove people to seek new lives outside their homeland.[10]

Critics focused on the issue of depressed wages in the United States.
Supposedly, American workers became part of the larger international
pool of labor once the country engaged in competitive trade. Workers
with few skills suffered the most because they were thrown into competition with their unskilled counterparts overseas. Their wages declined even if they did not lose their jobs to foreign workers.
Corporations, according to critics, coerced their employees into accepting lower wages by threatening to relocate abroad.

To this charge, free-trade enthusiasts replied that all benefits—not
solely hourly wages—should be included in determining compensation. For 1959 through 1995, according to the Brookings Institution,
increases in pay that included health-care coverage and retirement
benefits rose, since hourly wages tended to be static.[11] Data demonstrated that from 1959 through 1973, wages went up about 2.5 percent
per year but averaged only 1 percent after that point through 1995.
American productivity fell during the latter period, which explained
the slowdown in wages. Trade had little responsibility for slower rates
in wage growth, so the reply went, and may even have enhanced productivity with a beneficial effect on wages.[12]

Economists and statisticians presented a broad array of information to argue their cases for or against free trade. It had become such a feature of the American way of life that a return to protectionism was unrealistic. Consumers had grown accustomed to a vast assortment of goods produced overseas: automobiles, clothing, food, electronics, and many items used in industry beyond the sight of consumers. Because of the country's dependence on exports, the nation's economy could not withstand a loss of its markets. If the United States reduced its imports, it would soon have a reduction in exports, which had actually occurred for the pre–World War II generation. Dani Rodnik, a Harvard University economist, stated the difficulty of judging the merits of the interconnected economy: "There is no simple, single model of globalization."[13]

One indisputable accusation against globalization referred to the widening gap between rich and poor nations. Theoretically, free trade encouraged economic advancement for countries willing to participate in the international exchange of goods and services, which should bring an overall improvement in living standards. Proponents of free trade saw it as the most feasible way to fight poverty around the world as well as within particular countries. As far back as the Marshall Plan and the inauguration of GATT, business interests and theorists had justified the pursuit of foreign aid and reduced tariffs as steps toward trade development and ultimately the restoration of war-torn countries. Indeed, they cited the rising economic output of the world trading partners as proof of their position.

A flaw existed, however, that had significant implications for globalization and accounted in great part for the increased migration into the United States. Not all countries benefited from the new world economy, and even within the beneficiaries of global trade, the new wealth was not always distributed across the general population. In other words, the wealth generated by trade often went to elites, corporations, and the professional classes. In Third World countries, people on the lower rungs of the socioeconomic ladder missed out. "General disparities in wealth and income are rising rapidly," wrote Allen Hammond, director of strategic analysis of the World Resources Institute, "widening the gap between the rich regions and the poor ones."[14] During the twenty-year period 1970–1990, the per capita differences in income between developed and developing countries doubled.

Herein lay a serious concern of the world's economic leaders. The lack of opportunity accounted for the large migration of people into the United States and northern Europe. Resentment toward this large influx grew in both regions and created some ethnic strife. In a larger context, the lack of advancement among portions of the world population, whether in Latin America, Africa, or Asia, produced the likelihood of civil disobedience and political uprisings. Resentment toward the rich nearly always grew out of these conditions. Certainly the new telecommunications made the poor aware of their inferior status, which the literature on globalization recognized: "Economic disparities can also lead to despair and hopelessness or can help fuel anger and a sense of injustice that may add to emerging new security threats such as terrorism or crime targeting tourists."[15]

A major charge against globalization involved the exploitation of labor in poor nations, because trade improved the opportunity for developing countries to sell goods made by unskilled labor to the United States and other industrialized nations. This practice fit the theory of comparative advantage because it encouraged greater production in the United States by skilled labor for the export market. But critics insisted that since regional or world trade agreements failed to incorporate labor standards, the use of sweatshops and child labor grew since there was a natural desire to produce more goods for export. Corporations in undeveloped countries encountered little or no objection to their labor practices because the governments there wanted to export goods. Profits drove the transnationals to operate in the Third World where the political climate encouraged the lowest wages, so working conditions in those countries often reached deplorable depths. From the antiglobalists' stance, the interconnected world economy worsened poverty and violated human rights.

It was this issue—labor—that provoked much of the anger of the protestors in Seattle and at other sites of antiglobalism rioting. Developing countries strongly opposed any modification to the agreements, however, on the grounds that it would make them unable to compete in the world market. Poorer nations generally had little or no experience with labor standards or else showed little concern for the downtrodden. Protestors nonetheless held responsible all member nations of trade agreements, hoping to break down their negotiations over trade issues through demonstrations.

The provocative nature of labor exploitation made it an emotional topic. Advocates of free trade acknowledged the existence of sweatshops and child labor as well as the general abuse of workers, but they claimed that the United States was powerless to act until enough support materialized among member nations in groups such as the World Trade Organization to mandate improvements in working conditions. Trying to impose labor standards in developing countries could prove harmful because unfair wages still offered a better life for the impoverished. As one economist predicted, an effort to regulate or prohibit child labor would likely be revoked by the WTO since trade agreements tend not to "allow for discrimination among commodities or countries on the basis of differences in the mode of production."[16] Fear of economic imperialism disguised as labor standards caused developing countries to be skeptical and suspicious of proposals from rich nations on behalf of workers. Imposing such regulations in Third World countries might just leave workers destitute.

Overcoming the drawbacks and flaws of the world's labor practices probably reached beyond the ability of trade negotiators. Exploitation had existed prior to the growth of globalization, and the linkage between unfair labor practices and interconnected economies was not always clear. For this reason, defenders of globalization resorted to their original position that trade presented the best opportunity to raise living standards. Indeed, the desire to lessen people's dependence on relief and welfare served as a major force in the drive for encouraging international trade. Help for the poor and distressed more likely would require direct relief assistance, but even that tactic often succumbed to corruption and administrative inefficiency. "There is clearly a basic dilemma for the international community," wrote one analyst.[17] Migration remained the most feasible alternative to people trapped in dire circumstances.

The proponents of globalization who generally accepted David Ricardo's theory of comparative advantage saw immigration as a positive force in the U.S. economy. For them, immigration provided new sources of labor and a greater body of consumers, thereby resulting in economic gain. Economists explained that wage differentials between rich and poor nations served as the chief force driving people from one country to another. Therefore, since the United States had a robust economy and strong wages, it attracted workers, particularly from Latin America, who mostly took the low-skill and low-wage jobs. When a large number of immigrants come into the country, as was the case beginning in the 1970s, they depress wages, however, and may take away employment from local workers in low-skill jobs.

According to economic theory, the reduction of workers in the country of emigration will cause wages there to rise. The simple process of supply and demand prevails until equilibrium is set in wage scales. As one economist said, "The effect of labor mobility is thus to equalize wage rates in the two countries."[18]

Proponents of globalization acknowledged, however, that a simple application of the law of supply and demand did not recognize or explain all the factors and variables responsible for immigration. For it to work, "unrestricted labor mobility" must prevail, and migrants must encounter no costs in moving to another country. It also assumed that each migrant would find a higher-paying job. Moving into another country, according to Robert Carbaugh, has "economic and psychological costs," and "complete wage equalization may not occur."[19]

Carbaugh further explained that immigration, when viewed as labor mobility, increased the world's economic output because migrant workers in developed countries were more productive, since their new higher wage reflected a greater value of labor. Greater productivity might result, too, from the use of superior technology or the availability of immeasurable factors such as improved public health and transportation services. Regardless of the reasons, if immigrants increased their labor productivity by virtue of changing their country of residence, they would enhance the global value of goods and services. World output would grow.[20]

Other economists pointed to the effects of immigration on distribution of income. No one claimed that the benefits of the workers' increased productivity spread evenly around the world. Developed countries such as the United States who received large numbers of new arrivals gained by having a larger labor pool, because that enabled investors to maximize the use of capital. To be sure, American workers displaced by immigrants suffered, but the value derived from the extra labor provided by immigrants and their lower wages flowed to investors. Greater supplies of capital theoretically brought greater investment and more jobs. Displaced workers must learn new skills. The country supplying the new laborers tended to lose because its outflow of workers and increased wage scales meant less capital.

Defenders of globalization believe that immigration increases world output for reasons other than a growth in capital. For one thing, immigrants tended to send money to their families at home, which furnished badly needed dollars for their native country to use in foreign exchange. Immigrants, they also claimed, increased the diversity of consumer goods by introducing items from their own culture into the U.S. economy.

Heated differences of opinion arose nonetheless over the question of immigrants and welfare. Restrictionists claimed that a large number of immigrants became dependent on state and local welfare, thus adding to the burden of public costs. This pattern became true in the latter twentieth century with the large influx of impoverished immigrants from Latin America and Asia. In 1993, California, faced with a surging population of new arrivals, requested federal assistance in funding expenses incurred by services to immigrants. Governor Pete Wilson proposed a constitutional amendment changing the requirements for U.S. citizenship. Restrictionists believed that dependence on welfare discouraged the work ethic and passed a sense of dependency on to the next generation. Relying on local studies to bolster their case, restrictionists advocated a tighter control of immigration and more effective enforcement of existing laws. Indeed, better control of illegal migration across U.S. borders nearly always ranked near the top of their recommendations.

Activists for immigrants replied that the United States had a net economic gain because migrants' dependence on welfare was temporary, and once employed, they contributed to tax revenues. In 1997, for example, the National Academy of Sciences determined that an immigrant and his descendants paid over $80,000 in taxes above the cost of public services that they consumed during their lifetime.[21] Activists on behalf of immigrants conceded, however, that low-skill locals lost jobs or accepted poorer wages owing to cheaper immigrant labor.

A precise accounting of the cost/benefit ratio of immigrant labor may not prove possible, because immigrants and their families touch so many parts of the socioeconomic structure, such as schools, transportation, and public health and medical care. The fact that immigrants, particularly those entering illegally, depend on the underground economy compounded the confusion. The "impact on the U.S. of the wave of undocumented workers is beyond calculation," reported one news magazine.[22]

By the mid-1990s a new attitude toward illegal immigrants had emerged. Because of the great number of new arrivals coming into the United States, particularly into southern California, Texas, Florida, and New York, resentment began to grow over their use of public services. Californians complained about crowded schools, overloaded welfare rolls, and unpaid medical care. Throughout the country the belief grew that foreigners exploited the immigration system and abused public services. When terrorists who had remained in New York as aliens bombed the World Trade Center in 1993, the anger toward alien residents deepened.

In 1994 this anger erupted in California with Proposition 187, a state initiative approved by 59 percent of the voters. Although state and federal courts quickly issued injunctions against the initiative based on constitutional grounds, it would have kept the children of illegal immigrants out of public schools and blocked illegals' access to welfare as well as to health services, except for emergencies. Administrators such as school officials, medical doctors, and welfare officers would have to report suspected aliens.

Californians appeared to harbor the greatest resentment because their state had taken the largest number of immigrants from both Latin America and Asia. As described by one writer, California, the "land of endless summer," had begun to experience the end of the prolonged boom that had started in World War II. By the 1970s, the most populous state in the Union had crowded suburbs, congested traffic, severe pollution, a high crime rate, racial tension, and an aging infrastructure. These conditions worsened with the burden of several million immigrants, regardless of their status. For a while in the 1980s and 1990s, the Golden State had a net loss of population as middle-class whites fled to other regions, mostly to the Northwest, Colorado, and Texas. Proposition 187 represented much of the anger and frustration of the populace.

More than anger, however, lay behind the effort to restrict services. A genuine reevaluation of America's openness seemed to be under way. In 1986 the federal government, through the Immigration Reform and Control Act, granted amnesty to many illegal aliens employed in the United States, but the measure imposed stiff penalties for employers hiring undocumented workers. Issues over the correlation of immigrants with poverty, welfare, income inequality, and depressed wages captured more attention during the 1990s. One organization urging restrictions on the flow of immigrants claimed that the "growth in immigration-related poverty accounted for the lion's share (75 percent) of the total increase in the poor population between 1989 and 1997."[23]

Disagreements over immigration extended to a level beyond economics. Restrictionists invoked the ideals of American freedom and progress, asserting that large-scale immigration threatened the fabric of society. Advocates of immigrants' interests responded that closing the door would lead to stagnation and the loss of U.S. leadership in the world. Questions over race, nationality, and ethnicity rose to the top of the debate, giving immigration special importance among the forces responsible for the global diversity of the country. In this respect the issue resembled the arguments over immigration throughout U.S. history, when some Americans warned of impending danger while others saw newcomers as the source of strength in a democratic society. For example, warning that America faced the loss of its purity and its character because of the hordes of southern and eastern Europeans flooding into the nation, Madison Grant published in 1916 his famous call for restriction, *The Passing of the Great Race.* The United States stood in danger of being mongrelized, he insisted, by the predominantly Catholic or Jewish immigrants of the early twentieth century. Calls to save the Nordic race were not uncommon. It was this atmosphere of concern and anxiety that shut the door in 1924 to all except northern Europeans.

In 1924 restrictionists prevailed because of a different kind of American leadership. It was the age of protectionism, a time of retrenching and guarding the gate. Walls went up to keep out immigrants just as tariffs blocked foreign manufactures. In the context of globalization and the United States, this environment of protectionism contrasted with the social openness and free-trade credo after World War II. Since that point, the country's commitment to trade without barriers, to technological advancement, to full employment, and to equality for all races encouraged a freer attitude toward immigration.

The issue of lower wages and other dimensions of immigration erupted during the 2000 presidential election. In that year, Pat Buchanan of the Reform Party called for tighter control of borders and a more restrictive policy. He wanted to "cut back legal immigration to 250,000 per year" and "defend America's borders, if necessary with American troops."[24] Buchanan also intended to make English the official language of the United States and to initiate a national campaign to assimilate immigrants into U.S. "culture, history, and traditions." Buchanan's point of view, which had considerable support, grew out of the large influx of new arrivals since the reform act of 1965. Buchanan expressed the growing anxiety that immigration was endangering America's unity and sense of purpose.

Buchanan represented a more restrictive and isolationist position toward U.S. leadership in the world. For him and his followers, the country had overextended itself militarily, diplomatically, and economically. Too often American interests had been sacrificed for the sake of global organizations such as the United Nations, the World Bank, and the World Trade Organization. Too many entanglements, he contended, were disruptive and injurious to the best interests of the nation. His call for limited immigration blended well with the recommendation for a smaller role in world affairs. Buchanan also expressed the concern that globalization in this context harmed U.S. interests because the country was losing its sovereignty to world organizations. Loss of sovereignty to globalization had become an issue with antiglobalists just as the question of immigration had aroused public concern. "This then is a millennial struggle that succeeds the Cold War," he stated. "It is the struggle of patriots of every nation against a world government where all nations yield up their sovereignty and fade away."[25] Buchanan did not speak alone but reflected the sentiment that globalization, which included large-scale immigration of the last quarter-century, should be reversed or at least more closely regulated.

The views of Buchanan and the Reform Party did not prevail in 2000. Presidential winner George W. Bush, a proponent of free trade, took a different approach on immigration. He agreed that fluency in English was essential for success in the United States but saw the value of bilingual education. "The standard is English literacy and the goal is equal opportunity," he stated during the campaign, "all in an atmosphere where every heritage is respected and celebrated." As a presidential aspirant he recommended that the INS undertake reforms to reduce to six months the time for processing immigration applications, which usually took from three to five years. In regard to Latino immigration, the prime source of discontent for anti-immigrationists, Bush thought that the newcomers enriched the country "with faith in God, a strong ethic of work, community and responsibility." For him, "immigration is not a problem to be solved, it is the sign of a successful nation." From his pulpit as the leader of the Republican Party in 2000, he believed that "new Americans" should be "welcomed as neighbors and not feared as strangers."[26]

Democratic candidate Albert Gore also regarded English as essential for success in the United States, but he did not support "English only" proposals and laws. As vice president he had initiated a program for speeding up the process of applying for citizenship. Although controversial, the program enabled about 1.2 million applicants to obtain citizenship in a reduced time. Like Bush, Vice President Gore saw a rich heritage in immigration: "It is what has made us a great nation."[27] The fact that the presidential nominees of both major parties in 2000 endorsed immigration meant that openness prevailed over restriction, but the election of 2000 served nonetheless as an occasion for opposing views to be heard.

Activists for immigration generally concentrated on humanitarian considerations, emphasizing the nation's responsibility to offer economic opportunity to the downtrodden or invoking the emotional appeal of reuniting families. They exposed cases of discrimination and job bias. They lobbied legislators for amendments to policy or engaged in fund-raising benefits for destitute workers. Most of their activities centered on the practical and immediate side of immigrant life: food, housing, medical care, education, and employment. The justification for maintaining America's open door has, however, included broad statements that immigration is essential for the nation's political and economic health. Such proponents saw globalization as more than a matter of economics; it included cultural derivatives and humanistic values that only immigration could provide.

For Pascal Zachary, a global process of mixing races, ethnic groups, and nationalities was already under way that would redefine nations and world power. This development was "no passing fashion but a deep change." Zachary referred to persons of mixed race or ethnicity as "hybrids" and gave them great importance "in the intensifying global competition for trade and technology, wealth and jobs."[28] Migration across borders, he urged, should be encouraged and racial mixing accepted.

Zachary thought that hybridity was superior to diversity, that "pure is passé" and "original is out." Those nations with a high number of racial hybrids would be globalism's winners. America's world leadership and global competitiveness rested on its diversity, he claimed; "the new American is actively, creatively, sincerely and positively mongrel."[29] This social philosophy contrasted sharply with the sentiment expressed by Madison Grant in 1916.

Thus, in the development of globalization, migration played an important role in the United States after a new policy went into effect in 1965. Because of the restrictive nature of federal policy prior to that year, based largely on the quota system inaugurated in 1924, the liberalism of the latter twentieth century had an especially visible impact.

So large was the influx of newcomers that they were described as the "second wave." Asians and Latinos made up the largest portion of the new arrivals, who came mostly, but not entirely, for economic reasons. They increased the labor pool, and industries such as construction and agriculture became dependent on them. By concentrating their settlement in certain areas, they created neighborhoods or cultural enclaves that made their presence even more visible. Their demographic impact was significant enough by 2000 to stir resentment and anger, even to the point that immigration became an issue in the presidential race.

Although the official position on immigration remained largely unchanged in the United States at the new millennium, a growing sense of concern was evident. Urgent appeals for revising immigration policy, and particularly for strengthening and improving the operations of the INS, became increasingly popular. For the United States, Mexico presented the greatest challenge with illegal migrants. Mexico's growing population, which outstripped its economic base, had to find an outlet, and the United States continued to serve that function. Economic development remained the most feasible step for Mexico's displaced workers, meaning that U.S. efforts to reduce the surge of persons crossing its southern border would be only partially successful. If anything, the pursuit of trade embodied in NAFTA encouraged the flow of workers across the boundary. Moreover, the emotional appeal of uniting family members made a major revision of policy difficult to achieve. "Shifts in immigration policy," according to one writer, "generally have followed shifts in the political landscape."[30] Until a dramatic change in both the social and political atmosphere occurs, immigration policy will not likely undergo a major change. Some tightening of enforcement and adjustments in laws should be expected, but no restrictive legislation along the lines of the 1924 quota appear likely.

Countries in Europe, particularly Germany, faced a similar situation. In the post–World War II era, so-called guest workers were recruited to help rebuild the economy, and immigrants from southern Europe, especially Turks, moved into the northern countries. By the 1990s anti-immigrant sentiment surfaced in Germany and its government imposed some qualifications for immigrants, but in 2002 it remained a nation still accepting new workers. Globalization of the European economy ranked among the recognized causes of the large-scale immigration there.[31]

The European experience demonstrated that economic globalization encouraged migration. These two forces became inseparable, reinforcing and enhancing one another so that efforts to impose severe restrictions on immigration conflicted with the practice of open trade. As long as the United States remains an economic power and pursues a liberal trade order, immigration, even if illegal, will continue on a large scale. As people yearn for a better life, for adequate food and shelter, clothing, medical care, and opportunity, they will migrate. "The larger global context was now forcing its way into the daily lives of Americans," noted a political scientist. "Americans now had to recognize the relationship between their own traditions and those of the rest of the world, rather than ignoring the latter in a world of fixed borders around the country."[32]

NOTES

1. *The Economist* (November 2, 2002): 3.
2. G. Pascal Zachary, "New Cosmopolitans," *Deutschland* 6 (December 1999–January 2000): 64.
3. Patrick J. Buchanan, *The Death of the West: How Dying Populations and Immigrant Invasions Imperil Our Country and Civilization* (New York: Thomas Dunne Books, 2002), 3.
4. Roger Daniels, *American Immigration: A Student Companion* (Oxford, Eng.: Oxford University Press, 2001), 15.
5. "Relief from Illegals? Perhaps in 50 Years," *U.S. News & World Report* (March 7, 1983): 44.
6. Immigration and Naturalization Service, http://www.ins.usdoj.gov/graphics/aboutins/statistics/illegalalien/illegal.pdf, 2002.
7. Roger Daniels, "Changes in Immigration Law and Nativism since 1924," in *The History of Immigration of Asian Americans*, ed. Franklin Ng (New York: Garland, 1998), 82.
8. Immigration and Naturalization Service, http://www.ins.usdoj.gov/graphics/aboutins/statistics/299.htm, p. 1.
9. Daniels, *American Immigration*, 40.
10. Jerry Mander, "Facing the Rising Tide," in *The Case against the Global Economy and for a Turn toward the Local*, ed. Jerry Mander and Edward Goldsmith (San Francisco: Sierra Club Books, 1996), 8.
11. Burtless et al., *Globaphobia*, 60–88.
12. Ibid., 63–64.
13. *New York Times*, February 9, 2002.
14. Hammond, *Which World?*, 79.
15. Ibid., 81–82.
16. Dani Rodrik, *Has Globalization Gone Too Far?* (Washington, DC: Institute for International Economics, 1997), 32.
17. Dicken, *Global Shift*, 465.
18. Carbaugh, *International Economics*, 338.
19. Ibid.
20. Ibid., 339.

21. Sarah Anderson, John Cavanaugh, Thea Lea, and the Institute for Policy Studies, *Field Guide to the Global Economy* (New York: The New Press, 2000), 59.

22. "Invasion from Mexico: It Just Keeps Growing," *U.S. News & World Report* (March 7, 1983): 37.

23. Donald Coerver and Linda B. Hall, *Tangled Destinies: Latin America and the United States* (Albuquerque: University of New Mexico Press, 1999), 201; quote in Immigration and Poverty, http://www.fairus.org/html/04169910.htm, p. 1, 2002.

24. Original quote appeared in *San Francisco Examiner*, October 27, 2000, cited in http://www.issues2000.org/Celeb/Pat_Buchanan_Immigration.htm, 2002.

25. Pat Buchanan on Foreign Policy, http://www.issues2000.org/Celeb/Pat_Buchanan_Foreign_Policy.htm, p. 4, 2002.

26. Issues 2001, http://www.issues2000.org/Celeb/George_W_Bush_Immigration.htm, p. 1, 2002.

27. Issues 2001, http://www.issues2000.org/Al_Gore_Immigration.htm, p. 1, 2002.

28. G. Pascal Zachary, *Global Me: New Cosmopolitans and the Competitive Edge, Picking Winners and Losers* (New York: Public Affairs, 2000), ix, xix.

29. Ibid., xi.

30. Robert Suro, *Watching America's Door: The Immigrant Backlash and the New Policy Debate* (New York: Twentieth Century Fund Press, 1996), 7.

31. Klaus J. Bade, "The German Hub: Migration in History and the Present," *Deutschland* 6 (December 1999–January 2000): 38–43.

32. Edward S. Cohen, *The Politics of Globalization in the United States* (Washington, DC: Georgetown University Press, 2001), 154.

6 The Cultural Impact

Globalization promotes cultural diversity in those areas where the forces of the integrated world economy are most established. Globalization and culture, according to one writer, have a " reciprocal relationship," and "globalization lies at the heart of modern culture; cultural practices lie at the heart of globalization."[1] The United States has long regarded itself as a "melting pot" of people from different areas of the world with different ethnic and religious beliefs and practices, implying assimilation. During the past quarter-century, the term "salad bowl" has emerged to describe American culture as affected by the wave of immigrants: new arrivals have retained many of their old customs while living here. Regardless of terminology, the United States has been both recipient and purveyor of global cultural change, even to the extent that complaints arose within the country over the lifestyles of immigrants. But the most vocal expressions of dissatisfaction have come from spokespersons of other countries who denounced the spread of American culture around the world. So extensive has been this spread that it has been called "McDonaldization," meaning that a crass Americanism is replacing indigent cultures in foreign lands. Among some Europeans, globalization has meant Americanization.

Few cultural practices influence and affect behavior as much as language, and the fact that English now has become known as the "global language" indicates the role of the United States in globalization. Indeed, the growth of the integrated world economy and the leadership role of the United States paralleled the rising use of American English. "In 1950, any notion of English as a true world language was but a dim, shadowy, theoretical possibility," wrote one analyst, "surrounded by the political uncertainties of the Cold War, and lacking any clear definition or sense of direction. Fifty years on," he continued, "and World English exists as a political and cultural reality."[2]

The pervasion of English should not be regarded solely as American-driven, because nineteenth-century British imperialism accounted for the introduction of English to various parts of the world, including Australia, New Zealand, India, Hong Kong, and South Africa. Native populations in British colonies learned the language in formal classes, and the colonial governments conducted business in English. In some places such as the Philippines, the United States acted as a colonial power and imposed English on the locals, but it was not until the last half-century that the United States fostered the spread of English owing to its role as a military and economic superpower. American English flourished as a consequence of the U.S. struggle against communism, the expansion of its trade, and the huge growth of tourism. During the postcolonial era after World War II, when the use of English accelerated, the United States did not institute a policy of mandatory language but enjoyed the benefit of people voluntarily learning English in those countries where America's presence was most pronounced. For good reasons, one scholar wrote that "the present-day world status of English is primarily the result of two factors: the expansion of British colonial power, which peaked towards the end of the nineteenth century, and the emergence of the United States as the leading economic power of the twentieth century."[3]

Another consideration involved the timing of the Industrial Revolution. West European countries such as England, Germany, and France as well as the United States led the way. England, the home of the language, ranked at the forefront, and the United States started its march toward industrialization in the latter nineteenth century. These two industrial giants consequently engaged in much of the technological research and development, though not entirely, that later encouraged the spread of English. An Italian, Guglielmo Marconi, is credited with developing wireless telegraphy, or radio, in 1895, but its commercial use first occurred in the United States in 1920. Radio was an instant success as stations multiplied around the country. In the 1920s in Britain, radio grew under the aegis of the government via the British Broadcasting Company. Britain took the lead, however, in broadcasting to various countries, although not all programs were in English. Radio advanced, of course, in other countries regardless of language, but the commercial and industrial supremacy of the United States and

Britain in the interwar era brought a larger number of stations transmitting in English. In 1945 the infrastructure of the radio industry in English-speaking countries was well established.

A similar development occurred with the film industry. The early technology of movies advanced in non-English-speaking countries, but the devastation and losses imposed by World War II on Europe gave the United States and Britain the upper hand. Between the world wars the film industry moved forward with the leadership centered in the United States. With the addition of sound in the latter 1920s, language suddenly became an important dimension of movies, and English gained another foothold toward becoming the most common language around the world. As one writer explained, "When sound was added to the technology in the late 1920s, it was the English language which suddenly came to dominate the movie world."[4]

Other events and developments after World War I gave English an advantage in becoming more global. The conviction grew that the carnage of war required the creation of an international body to resolve disputes and maintaining world peace, and when the League of Nations went into operation in 1920, it made French—the traditional language of diplomacy—and English its two official languages.[5] The decision by the League of Nations to include English was likely owing to the impact of British colonialism; the first international body set in motion the growth of a global language. The Great Depression of the 1930s retarded trade and slowed the spread of English, but the global conflict of 1939–1945 left it poised to spring forward as the predominant language. In addition to the millions of soldiers engaged in combat around the world, the war left American military personnel occupying areas of Western Europe, Japan, and parts of Asia. The United Nations in 1945, like its predecessor, made English its official language. The Truman administration's extensive foreign aid programs such as the Marshall Plan, the beginning of U.S. hegemony, also encouraged American English to spread.

The growth of aviation was another factor. In 1951 the International Civil Aviation Organization (ICAO) established English as the official language for pilots and air controllers, known as "Airspeak." Obviously the airline industry needed a common language, and with the growth of tourism in the last fifty years of the century, Airspeak definitely promoted the international use of English. Some air disasters occurred owing to pronunciation errors and to accents of pilots whose native tongue was not English. Efforts to improve Airspeak have been made, however, and, regardless of the drawbacks, Airspeak pushed English.

The new technological developments in communications in the half-century after World War II built upon the advantages enjoyed by English-speaking countries. Computers and the Internet enhanced and promoted the language, although caution must be exercised when determining the number of international exchanges expressed in English. The fact remains that the United States led the world in developing the computer industry, including software. The U.S. Department of Defense's ARPANET, which later included commercial users, meant that new participants would have to resort to English. As the Internet grew around the world, the overwhelming amount of data loaded onto the system was in that language. Writers have clearly seen the dominance of English as the language of the "age of information," stating that it is "a force for global unity" and that "the more the network spreads, the more people are encouraged to learn English and the stronger the position of English becomes." Technology put English "in the right place at the right time."[6]

While the predominance of English owed much to electronic technology, the emergence of the United States as the sole superpower also accounted for the ascendency of English as the world's "global language." The country's vast military apparatus, which included numerous stations and bases abroad, and its gargantuan international trade in goods and services put American culture into nearly all parts of the world. Language accompanied the military and trade, and the widespread popularity of American radio, movies, and television thrust onto non-English-speaking peoples an unprecedented exposure to English. In order to accommodate American tourists or to deal with U.S. defense industry specialists, persons in other countries accepted the predominance of English and adapted to it. It has achieved status as an informal requisite among Third World aspirants for personal and economic improvement. According to one estimate, there were more people using English as a second language than native English speakers, meaning that there were about 2 billion users of the language by 2002, thus demonstrating the extent of the role of the United States in globalization.

The use of English, or the lack of it, became a major controversy in education in the United States during the latter twentieth century. Starting in the 1970s the federal government directed public schools to establish programs for helping students with limited skills in English.

In 1974 the Supreme Court issued such a ruling based on civil rights legislation, and in the following year the U.S. Department of Education recommended that schools provide multilingual classes. In 1981 the government removed the regulations imposed by the department, but bilingual instruction grew nonetheless as a step in education reform on the grounds that children of immigrants who spoke only their native tongue were at a disadvantage in English-only classes. In bilingual classes, students would allegedly advance as they acquired skill in the use of English. Some states, particularly California, had a large number of bilingual classes because of their steadily increasing immigrant population.

As immigrant populations grew, so did enclaves or neighborhoods of ethnic groups, especially Latinos, so that Spanish took over as the first language in small areas of the Southwest. The rising immigrant population and the influx of Spanish-speaking children in schools stirred concern in the United States. Latino activists called for the recognition of Spanish as an official language. Isolated incidents of small towns designating Spanish as the language for their city governments intensified the concern, and as some extreme Latino groups began to clamor for a predominant Latino culture—and even the creation of a separate and autonomous nation known as Aztlan in the Southwest—concern shifted to alarm among some Americans.[7]

It was this state of conditions that caused the rise of the English-only movement. In 1981 Senator S. I. Hayakawa introduced a proposal in Congress to amend the U.S. Constitution to make English the official language of the country, but he only persuaded the Senate to pass a resolution designating English. In 1996 the House of Representatives passed a bill requiring English to be the country's official language—a measure commonly known in Congress as the "Bill Emerson" bill because of his strong support for it. The Senate refused to take up the measure. Concern over the growing use of Spanish led in 1998 to the passage of Proposition 227 by California voters, which eliminated bilingual education in state schools. In 2000, Arizona voters approved a similar proposition; Colorado, however, voted down such an initiative in 2002, but Massachusetts approved one. A total of twenty-seven states had by that year passed legislation making English their official language even though they might continue bilingual education.

The large-scale immigration into the United States over the last twenty-five years was directly responsible for making language an issue in American culture. For some states the onslaught of school-aged children of immigrants into public schools became very burdensome, driving up costs and consuming resources that would otherwise be diverted elsewhere. From the view of the English-only advocates, a single language should prevail and immigrant children should learn English as quickly as possible. Latinos generally agreed that proficiency in English would expand their opportunities, but the dropout rate for their children was high. They claimed with some legitimacy that submersion into Anglo schools teaching only in English discouraged their children. Various organizations on both sides of the issue sprang up, such as U.S. English, English Language Political Action Committee, Federation for American Immigration Reform, Movimiento Estudiantil Chicano de Aztlan (MEChA), and La Vox de Aztlan.

One of globalizations's most significant consequences for world culture, with the United States again in the leadership role, was the triumph of capitalism over socialism because of the fall of the Soviet Union in 1991. The end of the Cold War left the open-market system of capitalism as the overwhelming economic force in the world. With the surge of the American economy in the 1990s, coming upon the heels of the Soviet Union's collapse, the Western democracies, particularly the United States, reinforced their claim that the way of life afforded by capitalism enhanced freedom of choice and encouraged the growth of democratic rights. Owing to the natural human desire for material well-being, people in countries previously oppressed by communism sought to be more productive and to engage in trade or barter. If communism failed, then economic progress, according to the capitalists, could be achieved through the open market. Even street vendors stimulated this growth as they engaged in small entrepreneurial operations. Described by one writer as "market exchange" practices and the desire for "barter and trade," the expansion of open-market transactions began to promote the spread of democratic culture.[8]

As this new cultural mindset grew in former Socialist and Communist countries that had, for example, been part of the Soviet bloc, a rising expectation of democratic rights followed. By 2002, capitalism penetrated areas of the world that had been closed and isolated for one half-century, and therein lay much of the potential for the global economy, an especially significant development for the United States with its vast resources and infrastructure for foreign trade. From this perspective, the Cold War amounted to more than a conflict over military power and ideologies; it was a clash over cultural behavior and attitudes not easily recognized but with nonetheless far-reaching consequences. "It had a social, as much as a military or political history," according to one authority.[9] In the final analysis the culture of freedom stood ready to grow alongside economic integration because economic freedom and personal freedom went hand in hand.

There is much disagreement, however, over the effects of the increasingly integrated world economy on culture. Antiglobalists see a march toward homogenization—global corporations overpowering small family-owned businesses that serve as the basis of a vibrant community. Writers of this persuasion regard globalization as "an ideology imposed on the world by transnational corporations and their followers in governments and universities."[10] Because of the sheer size of their operations, global corporations control "the flow of information, entertainment, culture, and basic ideas about what constitutes the good life."[11] When local culture is supplanted by larger outside forces, contend the antiglobalists, a slow deterioration follows in which crime, lower living standards, and urban decay flourish.

Other analysts who see the homogenizing effect of globalization on culture take a less acrimonious view. A certain amount of homogenization should be expected with the consumption of widely known products such as Coca-Cola or the common experience of seeing a popular movie. Sports generates a sense of familiarity among fans over star players and world events, with the Olympics and soccer as the obvious examples. Hence, a global consumer culture having similar characteristics may be found in countries engaged in world trade, but this degree of consumer homogeneity remains only at a superficial level.

Business transactions generated a common nomenclature among brokers dealing with the same commodity, especially those trading on the international market in oil or agricultural products. In order to participate in global trade, governments must also erect bureaucracies to handle the daily business of exporting and importing. A degree of homogenization thus becomes apparent and is known as the global marketplace. This development of similar practices rests on material goods and items of trade.

The United States has had the largest impact on homogenization owing to its predominance in the development of information technology. As American companies took the lead in advancing the technology of computer software, the Internet, satellites, and other technical aspects of modern communications, they gave the United States an enhanced position for affecting other cultures. It became "the leading producer of information products" in the "Information Age."[12] The rise of video entertainment enabled American movie and television production companies, because of their intact facilities and resources at the end of World War II, to distribute films in overseas markets. Entertainers and producers from other countries also penetrated the U.S. market. Whether through trade or entertainment, new technologies developed since 1945 provided the world's inhabitants with opportunities for sharing common experiences.

One of the major forces of cross-cultural pollination flows directly from higher education. Student foreign exchange programs developed by universities worldwide and the surge of foreign students studying in the United States over the last twenty-five years have enriched diversity. From as far back as the Middle Ages, academia relied on Latin as the universal language, which made possible the international character of universities in Paris, Bologna, Oxford, Cambridge, Prague, and Krakow.[13] During the nineteenth and early twentieth centuries, British, German, and French imperialism extended the influence of universities into various areas of the world and created a pro-Western culture among them.

During the latter nineteenth century, American colleges began to copy models of English and German schools. Students from the United States participated in foreign exchange programs prior to World War II, but these programs, for both Americans and non-Americans, tended to be small and elitist. After the end of the war the flow of students across borders began to increase, until by 2002 one educator could state: "The internationalization of higher ed in the last twenty years has been an enormous transformation of our enterprise."[14]

Several factors brought about this expansion of international study during the last half-century. With the launching of Sputnik in 1957 by the Soviet Union, the United States immediately bolstered its emphasis on education, especially on science and engineering, with the National Defense Education Act of 1958, as noted earlier. Thanks to this initiative sparked by the Cold War, federal funding for research enabled universities to offer new graduate programs that were attractive to foreign students. Simultaneously, the end of colonization ignited nationalism in the Third World, and the developing economies emerging along the Pacific Rim and in Africa, Asia, and the Middle East desperately needed skilled personnel. And the fall of communism in much of the world released young people for foreign study.

The United States offered the best resources in the fields of agriculture, engineering, science, business, and computer science. Petrodollars and the rising middle class in some Third World countries provided the funding for foreign students to study in the United States. They came as cash-paying customers, and by the 1990s many graduate programs became dependent upon them. In Europe, Latin America, and Asia, English served as the universal language in this international academic culture. Asians accounted for slightly over 50 percent of all foreign students enrolled in American universities during the academic year 1999–2000, according to the Institute of International Education (IIE).[15]

Alongside the emerging economies of the Third World was the affluence of the United States. The steadily increasing level of middle-class wealth in the country since 1945 enabled more families to afford a college education for their children, and with more women seeking formal education, the college student population of the United States mushroomed. Hence, a larger pool of students became available for study-abroad programs. Universities also sought to expand their curricula by offering cooperative programs with foreign institutions, and this combination of supply and demand made foreign study widespread in American universities and colleges. The IIE reported that over 143,000 American students were given credit for overseas studies in 1999–2000. Over the previous five-year period, enrollment of U.S. students in programs abroad climbed 61 percent. While Europe remained the most popular destination, the institute reported an increase in students traveling to Latin America, Asia, Africa, and the Middle East.[16]

Higher education thus became one of the most pervasive influences in the globalization of culture, and since 1945 the United States led the way. It published more journals than any other country; it offered more research and educational facilities, such as libraries and laboratories, and more financial aid; the economy allowed for part-time employment; and the open nature of American society appealed to many foreign students. Over 547,000 foreign students enrolled in U.S. universities and colleges in 2000–2001, a record total.[17] As American students went abroad, an exchange of cultures broadened their perspective and encouraged a camaraderie of scholars, a process greatly intensified by information technology. As affluence spreads and knowledge remains a pathway to social mobility, foreign study will become an even more regular feature of university matriculation. "In the knowledge-based society of the twenty-first century," stated one scholar, "the university will remain at the very center of economic and cultural development."[18]

Indicative of the new global culture was the rise of international sports, a development fostered by television. Media coverage helped to develop a universal sports culture replete with hero-athletes and global fans. As noted, the Olympics are the best example. The ancient Greek games were revived in the mid-nineteenth century but grew slowly until 1936, when fascist Germany used the Olympics held in Berlin as an international stage for propaganda. Because of the outbreak of war in Europe in 1939, the Olympics did not resume until 1948. By the 1952 games, in Helsinki, the Cold War had already begun and the Olympics were drawn into international politics. In 1956, Egypt, Lebanon, and Iraq boycotted the games over the Suez Crisis. In 1972, Palestinian terrorists took hostages at the Munich games and killed eleven athletes. And when the United States boycotted the 1980 event because of the Soviet invasion of Afghanistan and the Soviets retaliated with their own boycott of the 1984 games in Los Angeles, the Olympics had fully become a showcase for political causes.

Despite the pressure and tensions imposed on the Olympics by the Cold War and other disputes, they grew increasingly popular around the world. Global television broadcasts made possible by communications satellites launched in the 1960s and 1970s enabled millions of viewers to see them. Corporate sponsors gave the International Olympic Committee (IOC) funding. The spectacular opening and closing ceremonies and the alternating schedule for winter and summer events, for example, appealed to viewers, and so did the visual impact of athletes competing on an international scale and the ceremonial awarding of medals as the national anthem of the gold medalist was played. Olympic competition afforded visibility to smaller countries struggling for recognition. The Olympics thus succeeded in their original purpose: to promote peace and understanding on a global scale.

The United States also absorbed an international sport, soccer. Before it reached the United States, soccer was played in over 100 countries. The World Cup, the playoffs for the championship, was probably the single most popular world sports event; some stadiums in Europe held over 200,000 fans. Soccer began to grow in the United States during the 1970s with the development of mass communications. One of the first telecasts in the United States of the World Cup finals came in 1966, when England and Germany vied for the championship. Since then, soccer has spread across the country, and in 1968 the professional North American Soccer League (NASL) was started. The sport had a spurt of growth in the United States when Brazilian superstar Pele signed with the New York Cosmos in 1977.

Soccer quickly became part of American sports culture. It appealed to working-class youth who needed only a ball and open space. It was less violent than football and not prone to injure players, which appealed to mothers with school-age children, and it gave girls an opportunity to play sports without the need for excessive physical strength. An inexpensive sport, it required little in the way of equipment or special facilities. By 1985, however, the NASL had disbanded, and its member teams went to the Major Indoor Soccer League or became independent. A few professional teams stopped playing. At the secondary and collegiate levels, however, soccer continued to expand, with over 500 National Collegiate Athletic Association (NCAA) teams competing in 2002.

Soccer moved swiftly across borders only after technological advances made global telecasts possible, so that the surge of intercultural sports, whether the Olympics or soccer, coincided with the heightened economic activity by transnational communications corporations. This blend of technical and economic integration partly accounted for the perception of globalization as a development that began in the 1970s.

Despite the popular appeal of sports, however, nothing surpassed music as an agent of global culture. The United States has both exported and imported various styles, and the international music community constantly invents new ones. Rock 'n' roll, the most influential form generated in the United States since 1945, spread to Europe, Japan, and throughout other parts of the world. Some of America's most successful musical groups came, however, from overseas: the Beatles had the most impact on the United States. More recent styles include reggae and tejano. Other musical influences on a smaller scale in the last quarter-century have come from Brazil, Africa, and Argentina.

Two factors accounted for the growing diversity of music tastes: the rising pool of immigrants and the ease of obtaining foreign music through communications technology. Compared with the era soon after World War II, American music by 2002 was far more exotic and had greater ethnicity; musicians were less dependent on major recording studios for marketing because they could find a niche in the United

States. The post–World War II stress on civil rights also made white American tastes and practices less mainstream. Because of the new technologies, corporations such as Time-Warner, Sony, and Bertelsmann expanded the sale and distribution of music across borders and oceans and served as "carriers of culture and agents of socialization for whole generations of youth."[19]

If globalization accelerated the diversity of music in the United States, it had a similar effect in regard to food. In nearly all countries, food has a central place in the culture. The cuisine of France has, for example, a special status around the world. While American food has no comparable status, the United States offers one of the most varied diets and selections. This great diversity began with its early history because of the nature of colonization. The settlement of North America by Europeans—British, Dutch, German, French, and Spaniards—made the U.S. diet Eurocentric. Food became even more diverse with the arrival of the "New Immigrants" of the late nineteenth and early twentieth centuries. Nearly every region of the country reflected the impact of settlers and generations of new arrivals. In the South, for example, Creole cooking and the influence of African Americans stood out, just as the Mexican influence was apparent in the Southwest. If immigration continues on a large scale, more change should be expected in American food culture. However, the process of globalization after 1945 did not introduce radically new foods or bring a major shift in the American diet.

Nonetheless, the various features associated with globalization brought some new developments. Technology was responsible for the most change. Frozen food was available prior to World War II, but after the war it became a regular feature in grocery stores, owing partly to the inclusion of freezer compartments in home refrigerators. Fruits, vegetables, and meats could be stored for longer periods of time. This innovation, combined with high-speed jet aircraft, made possible the importation of exotic foods that previously were not obtainable. Fresh seafood such as crab and shellfish became readily available in the United States' interior. Some restaurants proudly featured menus based on seafood flown in from distant areas by jet.

The large influx of immigrants during the last quarter-century did not introduce new foods into the United States but had the effect of increasing their availability. This development was particularly true in regard to Latin America. Mexican food grew in popularity, and by 2002 it had become a regular feature on American menus. "So-called

Mexican food, including regional Mexican, Tex-Mex, New Mexican, Az-Mex, and Cal-Mex cuisine," according to one account, "boomed in the 1980s."[20] There was a demand for cookbooks describing Mexican and Spanish dishes. Tortillas, corn chips, and salsa became standard fare in the American diet.

A similar but less pronounced progression occurred with Asian foods. Due to the concentration of Asians on the West Coast and their smaller numbers compared with Latinos, the impact of Asian cuisines has not been as significant. A greater taste for items from China, Japan, India, and Vietnam nonetheless became apparent by 2002. American supermarket and grocery shelves commonly offer Asian foods, while Chinese food has found a niche in the restaurant industry.

Globalization also had an impact on eating habits by separating preparation from consumption. In other words, because of the availability of cold storage and rapid transportation, food may be processed in one area and shipped to customers in another area. Globalization encouraged consumers to rely on convenience foods and "fast food." Some analysts believed that globalization also promoted the homogenization of eating because cuisine became more standard. Known as "dietary transitions," the eating practices and types of food consumed changed as the residents of a country fell under a larger "foodshed" with the growth of integrated economies.[21] The media, whether through advertising or entertainment, helped drive the change in the dietary transition.

Globalization affected public health. The topic received considerable attention from governments, international bodies such as the World Health Organization, and private institutions. In 1996 the director general of the World Health Organization (WHO), Dr. Hiroshi Nakajima, warned of a "global crisis in infectious diseases."[22] The greatest threat came from tuberculosis (TB), diarrheal illnesses, malaria, and respiratory infections, which killed over 11 million in 1995 alone. Dr. Nakajima also warned that AIDS and Ebola posed new dangers, and he expressed concern over the "mad cow disease" outbreak in Britain and Europe that might affect humans through Creutzfeldt-Jakob disease. He pointed to the emergence of disease strains immune to treatment. A variety of reasons accounted for these developments, but he thought that international complacency over a reduction in infectious diseases because of the successes in eradicating smallpox and polio was responsible. A drop in cases of malaria and tuberculosis, which proved to be temporary, had encouraged this complacency.

Nearly all assessments of world health attributed the rise of infectious killers to poverty, civil unrest, and the lack of government attention. But health officials also noted levels of migration, ease of international travel, open borders encouraged by trade, and even climate change as factors. For the United States, the greatest threat came "from day-to-day movement of goods and people across our borders."[23] Human traffic across U.S. borders increased with improvements in travel and the wave of immigration just as the exchange of goods intensified with new trade treaties. "This flood of people and goods," reported the *San Francisco Chronicle*, "has exacerbated the job of controlling who and what enters and exits the nation."[24]

The potential threat of a crisis in world health rested on two considerations: the rise of infectious diseases around the world, and their rapid spread due to the forces of globalization. For the United States, its way of life was endangered by a recurrence of the "old diseases" such as tuberculosis and by the arrival of new killers by means of international travel and trade. One WHO study documented cases of communicable diseases such as measles and influenza contracted during travel on commercial aircraft and stated that "exposure to infectious TB on commercial aircraft is a real concern for both passengers and crew," although no confirmed cases had been made.[25] The seriousness of contracting tuberculosis prompted the WHO in 2001 to meet with airline representatives and public health officials and draw up guidelines.

In 2001 tuberculosis was the world's worst killer among infectious diseases, striking 3 million people per year. It infected as many as 8 million, but through treatment, or good luck, their cases never become active. During the late nineteenth and early twentieth centuries, tuberculosis raged as an epidemic in the United States and was overcome with a strong public health crusade. It continued to decline after World War II, but in 1985 the number of cases began climbing by about 20 percent per year. Tuberculosis began increasing in other areas of the world, too.

For the United States, tuberculosis rose in some respects as a side effect of globalization. The greater incidence of the disease came from immigrants, primarily Latinos and Asians. Since tuberculosis thrives in areas with poor housing, insufficient or unavailable medical care, and malnourishment, immigrants from developing countries have a proportionately higher rate of infection than U.S.-born citizens. Public health officials identified immigration from endemic areas such as

Latin America and Asia as a cause of the American increase. In 2002, Johns Hopkins University reported that "the impact of immigration of individuals from endemic areas had a notable effect in the United States."[26] In some parts of the United States, the rate of infection exceeded that in developing countries, justifying the WHO statement that "in an era of globalization, of increased travel and migration, the impact on the United States is direct."[27]

Intensifying the fight against the rising tide of tuberculosis was the emergence of drug-resistant strains, generally known as Multi-Drug Resistant TB (MDR-TB). Again, this development can be traced to the unregulated use of antibiotics in Third World sending countries. But tuberculosis strains also became resistant because of poor practices by patients in the United States who failed to follow the regimen of treatment. The disease was most common among the homeless and drug addicts. During the 1990s, forty-three states reported cases of drug-resistant tuberculosis. Immigrants accounted for 42 percent of the U.S. cases during the period from 1986 to 1998. Since they have limited access to health care, immigrants have come to be regarded as a major source of the threat.

Closely related to the question of tuberculosis's impact on public safety is AIDS. In many AIDS deaths, tuberculosis is listed as the immediate cause, but tuberculosis strikes those people with a decreased ability to fight disease. As AIDS patients lose their immune system, they fall prey to tuberculosis. To a great extent, AIDS is a disease generated in the United States without the influence of global migration.

Still, no better example illustrated the global nature of public health issues and their impact on the United States than AIDS. Questions arose over the origins of the disease when it emerged as a new killer in the early 1980s. First confined to Africa, it spread quickly around the globe and mystified the scientific world until it was isolated and identified in 1984. Its global nature—that is, moving across borders and onto continents—resembled the Black Death of the 1300s. Unlike patients with Ebola, who experience horrific hemorrhaging, AIDS patients appear normal during the early stages of infection, and the puzzling nature of the human immunodeficiency virus (HIV) that causes AIDS makes detection and control very difficult. AIDS spread fast owing to the advances of modern travel, but the nature of the integrated world economy contributed to its fast descent upon mankind. The appearance of AIDS coincided with the realization that the world had become an integrated circuit of economies and cultures. For good reason, wrote the president of the International AIDS Vaccine Initiative, "AIDS is the first widespread newly emergent infection of our globally interconnected era."[28]

On a global scale, the issue of AIDS divided between the rich and poor nations. For all countries, the number of HIV-infected persons climbed, but the ability to keep patients alive and productive was far superior in the developed countries. By 1996, nearly 22 million people worldwide lived with HIV/AIDS, but only 581,000 cases had been reported in the United States. The principal reasons accounting for the differences between rich and poor countries were related to health-care facilities: the lack of caretakers and treatment centers in poor nations. As an object of humanitarian concern, assistance from the developed countries provided the best chance for developing nations to make progress against AIDS.

The outlook for a radical improvement looked dim at the new millennium, with the likelihood that AIDS will spread even farther around the world. For the United States, the worldwide pandemic required caution and forbearance in the struggle against the encroaching disease. Precautions against infection became routine in the health-care industry, and extra steps to ensure safety became commonplace in all areas of health.

Therein lay another dimension to the impact of a dangerous global disease on the United States. The country had little security from the killer, and in view of the ongoing international travel and trade by Americans, the need for protection remained imperative. Diligence had to be exercised in daily life against AIDS. Globalization alone cannot account for the spread of AIDS, but the world nature of the U.S. economy and its increasingly varied culture made it more threatening to Americans.

One persistent world killer and debilitant is malaria, particularly in sub-Saharan Africa. Once a threat to U.S. public health, malaria was overcome with land improvement and eradication programs that occurred mostly prior to World War II. Indicative of the peril of mosquito-borne illnesses in the United States, however, was the 1999 outbreak of West Nile fever in the Northeast. In that year sixty-two cases broke out, with seven fatalities.[29] Birds carry the fever, but the origin of the West Nile outbreak likely came from a tourist returning from abroad. Malaria appeared from time to time in Paris because of the frequent flights from West Africa, and French airlines personnel commonly sprayed the cabins of aircraft with insecticides as a preventative measure. American carriers refused to take such measures on flights coming from tropical countries, but the threat remained. "Tiger mosquitoes arrived in the United States approximately twenty years ago, allegedly on a ship of old tires from Asia. These are the dangers of globalization," stated David Heymann of the WHO.[30]

In 1989 a public health issue arose in Europe over the human consumption of beef from animals fed in the United States with weight-gaining hormones. American farmers and ranchers had used hormone-intensified food for livestock for at least a generation, but the European Union blocked the importation of U.S. beef on the grounds of public safety. In this country, trade negotiators and agricultural interests saw the moratorium on American beef as a barrier to protect European farmers from competition. Again, no documented case of illness or death occurred, but the issue remained unresolved by 2002 as negotiators at the WTO continued to search for a solution.

With the start of the twenty-first century, Americans were adjusting to new developments in the religious makeup of the country. With a culture based on the ethic of white Anglo-Saxon Protestantism, the United States began to experience an increase in the followers of Islam, or Muslims. Islam had been a very minor religion here and drew little attention until the 1960s, when it began to grow among African Americans, giving rise to the Black Muslim movement. New converts liked the religion's emphasis on nonviolence, modesty, and prayer. In the turmoil of the civil rights uprisings of the 1960s, however, Muslims were suspect and their faith became associated with violence. In 1965 the assassination of Malcolm X, the leader of the Black Muslims, by a rival group within the denomination encouraged the perception of Muslims as being prone to violence. Islam continued to be regarded as an esoteric religion within a minority group.

Another dimension came with the increase of immigrants from Muslim countries in the Middle East. The new wealth in the region, based on petrodollars, starting in the 1970s gave rise to a new middle class, which encouraged education and travel. Arabs started to attend American universities and colleges, and some chose to stay in this country and become citizens. Political and civil unrest in the Middle East also drove Muslims to the New World, where they sought opportunity for advancement, much like previous generations of immigrants. By 2000, the number of Muslims, fueled by immigration, had reached nearly 6.8 million in the United States. By 2002, Islam was the fastest-growing religion in the United States. Mosques began to appear in neighborhoods along with the traditional churches and temples.

Americans started to show alarm over the growth of Islam in this country. The Iranian hostage crisis of the late 1970s stirred concern over the rise of fundamentalist Muslims and their hostility toward the United States. With terrorist bombings of aircraft by Islamic organizations, the 1993 bombing of the World Trade Center in New York, and finally the infamous terrorist attack on New York on September 11, 2001, worshippers of Islam were suddenly under suspicion, and law enforcement agencies investigated some Muslim leaders suspected of being terrorist supporters and organizers. A few incidents of violence against individual Muslims happened around the United States, but no widespread violence such as riots or mob action occurred.

The impact of Asians on American culture reached a new height by 2002 because of the Immigration Act of 1965. That measure, as we know, removed most of the restrictions on Asian migration into the United States, which led to a large influx. Compared with Muslims, Asians exhibited more diversity in their lives. Catholicism was a common religion among the Vietnamese and Filipinos, and they tended to be self-employed. Enclaves of Asians were formed in large cities, with neighborhoods populated almost entirely by a specific nationality. Los Angeles had Korea Town and Little Manila, while Little Saigon appeared in Orange County, California. As discussed in Chapter 5, Asian arrivals maintained their ethnic identity through religious contacts and the subculture of the enclave.

The concentrated pockets of Asian communities on the West Coast, where new languages and forms of behavior displaced American English and culture, heightened the controversy over English as the official language. As large numbers of Asian children entered the public schools, the controversy became more intense. Resentment also grew over the displacement of American workers by Asians willing to accept lower wages. This resentment of Asians erupted in the Los Angeles riots of 1992 that followed the police arrest and beating of Rodney King. During the riots, when African Americans protested the incident, they focused much of their anger on Korean businesses, burning and looting Korean-owned shops and stores. Black rioters complained that Koreans charged them high prices for food and other wares. However, for the rest of the 1990s, violence against ethnic groups subsided due to the high employment rate and growth in real wages.

On an international level, the subject of globalization and its cultural impact often led to the emotional issue of "McDonaldization." Critics of globalization saw McDonaldization as an intrusion of American commercialism into local cultures. Its goal was to replace them, so the argument went, with a homogenized lifestyle geared toward mass consumerism. Critics looked upon McDonald's hamburger outlets as the epitome of standardization as well as an insidious form of American domination around the world. "McDonald's fast-food restaurants and the process of McDonaldization are all largely, if not exclusively, American phenomena, at least in terms of their origin."[31]

In this context, McDonaldization became synonymous with the drawbacks of globalization, and it was chiefly a cultural effect resulting from the highly efficient, low-cost operations of a retail transnational headquartered in the United States. To be sure, the term went beyond fast food; it included standardized products marketed on a worldwide basis such as Coca-Cola. One of the first products to symbolize the export of American culture, Coca-Cola became a target of antiglobal critics. Other barbs were aimed at Starbucks coffee, Nike shoes, the Hard-Rock Cafe, and Disney theme parks. McDonaldization developed into a broad term encompassing the resentment toward the presence of American transnationals in foreign countries, but it also included the loss of any individual qualities of any culture wrought by the massive economic power of a global giant. McDonaldization nearly always referred to American intrusion into overseas markets that tended to homogenize the local culture. But critics complained that the same homogenizing influence was seen in the United States with fast-food outlets. Likewise, some observers regarded Wal-Mart as a global retailer that tended to drive out small-town competition by family-owned businesses, with a negative impact on local culture.

Despite the penetration of markets by American transnationals, the proliferation of fast-food chains and Hollywood movies, and the popularity of American blue jeans overseas, native and indigenous cultures remain entrenched. Economic integration did not, for example, slow the growth of nationalism in Third World countries, as seen in the rise of Pan Arabism, independence movements in the former Soviet bloc, or the quest for democratic governments in Latin America. Except for the most undemocratic societies, countries have continued to join the global trading bloc either through the WTO, NAFTA, the European Union, or other organizations. The United States stood accused of cultural imperialism, but it was impacted, too. Few cultures have absorbed as many foreign influences as the United States, which continues to invent and reinvent itself with sweeping waves of newcomers to the New World.

The country's large trade deficit, reaching nearly $500 billion in 2002, indicated the American desire for foreign goods. And the widespread practice of pegging currencies to the U.S. dollar created the "dollar standard" described as "an indispensable fount of liquidity for world trade."[32] Much of the standardization associated with globalization related to the consumption of products and the daily business of world trade, so that American "cultural imperialism," which leapt forward in 1945 because of the country's advantageous position at the end of World War II and in the subsequent Cold War, was the result of newly restored economies and their increased power in world trading blocs. As in the case of Europe, stated a culturalist, it led to "a process of cross fertilization, a reciprocal exchange of ideas about film-making and fashion, architecture and literary criticism, furnishings and food."[33]

A major change in American culture that began generally at the end of the 1950s but accelerated over the last twenty-five years was the end of the dominant culture, the mainstream value system based on the white Anglo-Saxon Protestant ethic. The country's new credo of civil rights and the political and economic empowerment of women and minorities were greatly responsible, but the impact of globalization also accounted for this decline. Large-scale immigration, particularly from Latino countries, induced by global economics brought a new concern and appreciation for Hispanic studies and the recognition of the Latino contribution to American history and culture. A similar development occurred on a smaller scale with the influx of Asian immigrants. Just as African Americans and women took a more powerful role in U.S. culture, so, too, have Latinos because of their rising numbers in the general population. "Indeed, the future of the United States," stated a scholarly analysis, "will be in no small measure linked to the fortunes of a heterogeneous blend of relatively recent arrivals from Asia, from the Caribbean, from other parts of the world, and above all from Latin America." The sheer size of the immigrant population warranted the assertion that "the United States is now in the midst of unprecedented change."[34]

The full ramifications of the new diverse culture remained unknown in 2002, but the integration of professional and collegiate sports, which included athletes from the Caribbean and Latin America, has become passé. In the political arena, the rise of Latino spokespersons and leaders at all levels of government will continue if the flow of immigrants from the south is maintained and if the general Hispanic community becomes more politically active. Educational reform should be expected in the design of new curricula not centered exclusively on Eurocentric history and culture. By 2000, a national debate was under way on whether to continue to teach Western Civilization as the foundation of U.S. culture.

Globalization obviously had an impact on America's own culture, just as its economic and cultural power affected other countries. As it delighted in seeing the spread of English around the world, the United States experienced a challenge to English within its own borders. Serious difficulties arose in public education, and new concerns emerged over public health with the rise of infectious diseases, both of which were traced to large-scale immigration. A growing sense of concern filled the air as political leaders, writers, and spokespersons for popular organizations warned of a threat to American culture. The general public demanded the assimilation of new arrivals while immigrant activists urged them to maintain their cultural autonomy and to fight for political separatism. Nonetheless, English became the first language of Latinos and other immigrants.[35] With its relentless force, globalization promoted the diversity of our country and broadened its culture. Such cultural change will continue in the United States and in all countries that remain our trading partners in the integrated world economy.

NOTES

1. John Tomlinson, *Globalization and Culture* (Chicago: University of Chicago Press, 1999), 1.
2. David Crystal, *English as a Global Language* (Cambridge, Eng.: Cambridge University Press, 1997), vii.
3. Ibid., 53.
4. Ibid., 90.
5. Ibid., 79.
6. Quotes appear in ibid., 107, 109, 111.
7. Buchanan, *The Death of the West*, 128–33; http://www.americanpatrol.com/MECHA/AZTLAN.html, p. 1, 2002.
8. Francis Fukuyama, "Economic Globlization and Culture," Merrill Lynch Forum, http://www.ml.com/woml/forum/global.htm, 2002.
9. Halliday, *The World at 2000*, 21.
10. Jay Walljasper, "Cultural Effects of Economic Globalization," *Conscious Choice* (July 1996): 2. Reprinted: http://www.consciouschoice.com/issues/cc094/economicglobal.html, 2002.

11. Ibid., 2.
12. David Rothkop, "In Praise of Cultural Imperialism: Effects of Globalization on Culture," *Foreign Policy* (June 22, 1997): 3, in http://www.globalpolicy.org/globaliz/cultural/globcult.htm, p. 3, 2002.
13. Philip G. Altbach, *Comparative Higher Education: Knowledge, the University, and Development* (Greenwich, CT: Ablex, 1998), 4.
14. *New York Times*, September 7, 2002.
15. http://www.bibl.u-szeged.hu/afik/opendoors_2000.html, p. 2, 2002; http://www.opendoorsweb.org/Press/International Students in the US. htm, p. 3, 2002.
16. http://www.opendoorsweb.org/Press/Americans Studying Abroad.htm, p. 3, 2002.
17. http://www.opendoorsweb.org/Press/International Students in the US. htm, p. 1, 2002.
18. Altbach, *Comparative Higher Education*, xvii.
19. Robert Burnett, *The Global Jukebox: The International Music Industry* (London: Routledge, 1996), 3.
20. Colin M. MacLachlan and William H. Beezley, *El Gran Pueblo: A Study of Greater Mexico*, 2d ed. (Upper Saddle River, NJ: Prentice-Hall, 1999), 483.
21. Jeffrey Sobel, "Food System Globalization: Eating Transformations and Nutrition Transitions," in *Food in Global History*, ed. Raymond Grew (Boulder, CO: Westview Press, 1999), 177–78.
22. Press Release, World Health Organization, http://www.who.int/whr/1996/press.html, 2002.
23. *San Francisco Chronicle*, January 6, 2002.
24. Ibid.
25. Executive Summary, http://www.who.int/gtb/publications/aircraft/summary.html, p. 1.
26. Diseases, http://www.hopkins-id.edu/diseases/tb/tb_epi-html, 2002.
27. Population Resource Center, The Globalization of Infectious Diseases, http://www.prcdc.org/summaries/disease/disease.html, p. 3.
28. Seth F. Berkley, "The Outlook for Eradicating AIDS," in *Critical Issues in Global Health,* ed. C. Everett Koop, Clarence E. Pearson, and M. Roy Schwarz (San Francisco: Jossey-Bass, 2001), 144.
29. *New York Times*, September 3, 2000.
30. Ibid.
31. George Ritzer, *The McDonaldization Thesis: Explorations and Extensions* (London: Sage Publications, 1998), 71.
32. *The Economist* (September 14, 2002): 74.
33. Pells, *Not Like Us*, 279.
34. Quotes in Marcelo M. Suárez-Orozoco and Mariela M. Páez, eds., *Latinos: Remaking America* (Berkeley: University of California Press, 2002), 1.
35. *New York Times*, April 7, 2002.

7 | The New Terrorism

When President Franklin D. Roosevelt asked Congress in 1941 to declare war against Japan, he described the surprise attack on Pearl Harbor as "a date which will live in infamy." Over one half-century later, on September 11, 2001, the terrorist assault on New York City burned into the American psyche as a new day of horror as over 3,000 persons died in the collapse of the twin towers of the World Trade Center and the strike against the Pentagon, the command center of the U.S. Armed Forces. Using commercial airliners as missiles, suicide hijackers flew directly into the buildings and a fourth airliner crashed into a rural Pennsylvania field as the passengers fought back. The total loss of life exceeded that at Pearl Harbor. Television viewers around the world watched these shocking scenes as they took place, including footage of people jumping from buildings. To describe the aftermath of the attack, reporters had to resort to the language of gruesome detail: "war zone," "crushed bodies," and "body parts." No event since World War II matched the widespread horror of the day now known as "9/11." So intense was the impact of this attack that Americans regarded it as a turning point in their personal lives as well as in the history of the United States.

This awful tragedy had global implications and ramifications. To begin with, the hijackers belonged to a worldwide network of terrorists known as al-Qaeda, based in the Middle East and led by Osama bin Laden. He was a Saudi Arabian considered by the United States to be responsible for an earlier bomb attack on the World Trade Center in 1993. Bin Laden and his followers took advantage of the same technologies of globalization used to promote trade, capital flows, international travel, and fast communications. "Computers and satellite phones have become standard equipment in terrorist groups," according to one assessment.[1] The terrorists converted a principal instrument of globalization, the commercial airliner, into a deadly weapon. Through his use of the Internet, Bin Laden and his cohorts had set up cells of terrorists around the world, keeping them organized and active with the electronic transfer of money and instructions for planning an attack. The effectiveness of his organization was astounding, for he was able to recruit members from various countries, although most were Middle Eastern, and disperse them throughout the United States and Europe, where they lived unobtrusively. Bin Laden's al-Qaeda resembled a transnational corporation in its structure, use of technology, and international impact. "For better or worse," stated one columnist, "the world has entered an era of networks."[2] Reflecting on the World Trade Center attack, a prominent German intellectual wrote that "it would be strange indeed if terrorism had not also gone global."[3]

A major consideration for the terrorists was the assurance of television coverage. In order to achieve the maximum impact, they needed publicity and media exposure on an international scale, and the destruction of the World Trade Center suited their purposes perfectly. Coverage of the disaster began immediately, sending horrific images of destruction and carnage into remote corners of the world. The technology of global communications—television in this case—gave their assault the sense of theater so essential for their success.

The global implications of terrorism reach beyond its organizational structure. Terrorist acts stretch far back into history, but in view of its worldwide organization, its dependence on "borderless" technologies, and its international scope of operations, al-Qaeda represented the new terrorism of the age of globalization. New terrorism arose alongside the development and emergence of the integrated world economy and the ascension of the United States to the post of global leader. Therein lay a critical point: the new global terrorists struck on a local level during the immediate post–World War II period as part of the Israeli-Palestinian conflict. In the beginning they tended to confine their violence to the Middle East, but starting in the 1970s they demonstrated their intent to expand more broadly.

In 1970 terrorists considered to be affiliated with the Palestine Liberation Organization (PLO) blew up a Swissair jet carrying forty-seven passengers and crew. In 1972, an Arab group known as Black September killed eleven members of the Israeli Olympics team during the Munich games. The United States fell within the crosshairs of the terrorists' aim in 1983 when a suicide bomber belonging to the Islamic Jihad drove a truck loaded with dynamite into the U.S. Marines barracks in Beirut, killing 241. Members of the PLO seized the Italian cruise ship *Achille Lauro* and murdered an American passenger in 1985. Americans had not become, of course, the only targets of terrorists, but they increasingly became victims. In 1988 a terrorist-planted bomb blew up Pan American Flight 103 over Lockerbie, Scotland, and killed 259.

It became evident in the 1990s that the United States had become the focused target of terrorists, or at least of Osama bin Laden. In 1993 a bomb exploded in the basement of the World Trade Center, killing six and injuring about 1,000. In 1998 the U.S. embassies in Kenya and Tanzania were bombed, killing twelve Americans and injuring about 5,000 employees. When the USS *Cole* was bombed in Yemen in 2000, killing seventeen sailors and wounding thirty-nine, it was clear the United States faced a new enemy. With the attack on New York about one year later, intelligence and law enforcement agencies had no doubt that Bin Laden had organized a jihad, or holy war, against the United States.

In 1995, Benjamin R. Berber published *Jihad vs. McWorld*, in which he described an emerging conflict between the commercialism of the West and the opponents to modernization among fundamental Muslims: "Nowhere is the tension between democracy and Jihad more evident than in the Islamic world, where the idea of Jihad has a home of birth but certainly not an exclusive patent." For Berber, a global conflict was under way between Jihad's "bloody politics of identity" and McWorld's "bloodless economics of profit."[4] Only through a renewed commitment to individualism and civic virtues did Berber think the world could maintain its hope to extend democracy.

Connecting the Islamic jihad with globalization is not unreasonable. Muslim fundamentalists made their dislike for Americans very clear, for they regarded the United States as a declining power with a decadent culture. They saw America's hegemony in the Middle East as a threat to the moral fiber of the Muslim world, whether it protected its own interests, particularly the oil resources there, or served as an ally of Israel. The affluent West, led by an overbearing United States, has a culture indulgent in materialism and promiscuity and willing to exploit others in order to satisfy its own greed. Americans allegedly have no respect for the beliefs and values inherent in Islam and regard it as a hindrance in their drive for control of oil in the Middle East. Particularly offensive to fundamentalist Muslims were media and entertainment productions that, in their eyes, debased women and glorified violence. This view of the United States spread across many Muslim countries, where the revulsion against America remained deeply rooted among fundamentalists.

By the same token, Americans had a negative view of Muslim fundamentalists and certain features of Middle Eastern culture. In those Islamic countries ruled by fundamentalists, the United States regarded oppression of the common people and a lack of respect for human rights as undemocratic and uncivilized; dictators or regimes of elites endangered life and liberty. Americans looked upon the former Taliban rulers in Afghanistan, which sponsored al-Qaeda, as barbaric. In the United States, where a surge of social reform for women's rights has been under way for two generations, the forced wearing of burqas by Muslim women was considered repulsive. From the American perspective the extreme poverty common in the Middle East resulted from the oppressive social and political climate because it killed innovation and stifled an economics of choice. Acceptance and admiration of Islamic suicide terrorists, who become martyrs in their hometowns, remained an alien concept.

As perceived in the United States, the September attack required a global response. A conflict of ideologies and cultures rooted in religious beliefs and perceptions of human value had emerged. For Americans, terrorism spawned an ethical dimension to globalization, and a new moral imperative seized the country, one that demanded the eradication of terrorism and threats to the American way of life. To fight this battle, the United States intended to use the weapons of globalization: communications, aircraft, its own network of intelligence resources, and foreign aid. From its view, the attack on New York and the Pentagon left no choice. The annihilation of Bin Laden and his al-Qaeda became only the first step in a worldwide campaign to be fought on behalf of all people subject to the threat of terrorism. A careful distinction was made, however, from the beginning: only terrorists would be targeted and not Muslims per se or Islam in general. In the minds of U.S. policymakers, this distinction was an important contrast to Bin Laden's random violence against Americans.

The new terrorism of globalization produced a series of immediate changes in the daily lives of Americans. Security became the overriding consideration at airports. Inspections of baggage and personal checks for weapons became more thorough, and armed National Guard troops were stationed at many airports. Travelers now had to arrive much earlier for their flights because of the long lines at clearance points. Similar precautions were taken at large mass gatherings, and considerable effort was expended for security at the 2002 Super Bowl and Winter Olympics. Fighter jets patrolled the skies over large cities for several months after the attack in order to prevent further terrorist strikes by airliners. The severity of the situation became clear when the public learned that fighter pilots were authorized to shoot down any commercial airliner, regardless of the nationality of the passengers, if it appeared to be hijacked. At first only the President of the United States had the authority to issue such an order, but it was delegated to high-ranking military officers later. Schools and businesses established evacuation plans. The American people accepted the inconvenience of long waiting lines and searches of their luggage.

Less tangible but equally important shifts in attitudes occurred. A surge of patriotism permeated the United States as people wished to express their confidence in the U.S. government. Military recruiters reported a higher rate of enlistment. Flag waving and personal displays of patriotism became common. Little evidence of jingoism surfaced, but a new popular attitude toward government appeared, in contrast to the general antifederal opinion in vogue since the end of the Vietnam War. Americans realized they were no longer isolated from world terrorism and that their interoceanic position in North America no longer protected them. The awareness grew that each person was vulnerable to fanatical groups on the other side of the world. Even though the Cold War had previously demonstrated their geographic vulnerability, a new generation rediscovered it on September 11.

The September attack forced the people of the United States to recognize and acknowledge the seriousness of the new terrorism, which had been in a state of growth and development since World War II. After the war, conflicts around the world sparked the emergence of terrorists and guerrilla fighters for various causes and political movements; they fought in postcolonial struggles for independence or in renewed ethnic and religious feuds. Among the better-known areas of conflict were Northern Ireland, North Africa, the Balkans, and Southeast Asia. During the Cold War the Soviet Union often supplied leftist organizations with weapons and funds. Moscow depended on

Communist Cuba under the leadership of Fidel Castro, for example, to serve as a base of operations for guerrilla warfare in Latin America.

Proliferation of arms during the Cold War enabled small bands of fighters and terrorists to obtain weapons, and the continued sale of arms in the 1990s by major powers, including the United States and former states of the Soviet Union, kept the supply forthcoming. Arms usually followed a circuitous route on their way to terrorist strong-holds, but the worldwide market made, and continues to make, the acquisition of weapons easy. The Middle East provided the most fertile ground for terrorism, where the conflict between Arabs and Jews had all the major elements for the development of terrorism: territorial squabbles, ethnic identities, religious fanaticism, and deeply rooted cultural differences.

Under these conditions the chronology, technology, and organization of terrorism in the Middle East followed a pattern similar to globalization: it began soon after World War II; it was caught in the conflict between the superpowers, described in one case as a "proxy war"; it reached beyond its original parameters of activity and started operating on an international scale in the 1970s; it relied on the new technologies of globalism; and it developed an organizational network similar to a transnational corporation. Not to be overlooked was the growth of nationalism, or Pan Arabism, in a region long dominated by European colonial powers.

Another form of destructive activity is cyberterrorism. Computer hackers and developers of "viruses" have caused temporary shutdowns of computer and Internet services and destroyed data, though not on a worldwide basis. Such terrorism threatened air traffic control and endangered lives. To protect sensitive data and communications, government agencies and private companies employed encoding systems similar to secret codes used in the past, but a new software known as Echelon can decipher encoded data. Another controversial software product was Carnivore, which enabled law enforcement agencies to tap e-mail messages much like a telephone tap.

The ghastly attack on the World Trade Center renewed the country's sense of global mission. Almost overnight, political leaders, with widespread support, announced their intention to strike back at the terrorist organization responsible and to take the fight to terrorists everywhere. This goal included striking at those governments sponsoring or harboring terrorists. Throughout the United States, people welcomed this stance with enthusiasm; approval ratings for President

George W. Bush rose to 86 percent. Not since the commitment to oppose communism in the early stages of the Cold War had public support been as united and focused. A new common purpose blended patriotism and military action with a determination to defend American culture. Americans understood the global nature of the struggle— that the new terrorism was not confined to one country or opposing government but had spread throughout the Arab world and even among its allies there. In Egypt, Saudi Arabia, Pakistan, and non-Arabic Muslim countries such as Indonesia, there existed a desire to reduce American omnipresence. To overcome such hostility, the United States believed that it had to take military action against terrorists and to extend foreign aid and goodwill into those areas where resentment festered. "This is the world's fight," President Bush stated in his special address to the nation. "This is the fight of all who believe in progress and pluralism, tolerance and freedom."[5]

The terrorist attack had an immediate impact on trade—the cornerstone of globalization—but the effects proved to be minor. Even though the hijackers hoped to disrupt international commerce by striking the World Trade Center, ironically the business practices induced by globalization lessened the impact. To be sure, the terrorist outrage of September 11 forced adjustments and delays in the shipping industry. Carriers such as United Parcel Service (UPS) had to reroute some cargoes because the Federal Aviation Service prohibited freight on passenger aircraft. Large-scale retailers had to prioritize items they wanted delivered, but no shortages appeared on stock shelves. Some cutbacks and delays occurred with oceanic shippers, but again the impact on supply was minimal. Bottlenecks and delays at border checkpoints developed because of security inspections, but no serious lack of goods and supplies ensued. Like passengers waiting to board commercial jets, the worst feature was the inconvenience of waiting.

Trade organizations such as the Asia Pacific Economic Cooperation (APEC), the Pacific Rim group, began to incorporate security measures into their operations. Member companies had to learn to share intelligence, for example, among themselves and with law enforcement agencies. It became necessary to tighten inventory controls and verify the safety of cargoes. Political instability and terrorist threats thus became a new concern for organizations that previously had only focused on the interchange and logistics of shipping.

The airline industry and tourism sustained a major setback as people cancelled flights or took alternate means of transportation.

Obviously, the emotional impact of the World Trade Center attack and the scenes of death and destruction, replayed on television, made people fearful or cautious about air travel. By the six-months' observance of the attack, in March 2002, airline passenger traffic had begun to rebound and reached about 80 percent of its pre-attack level.

Tourism, the world's largest and highly globalized industry, immediately experienced a severe downturn in business and felt a sense of alarm. "The crisis is a global one, but it must be managed on a local basis," stated Egyptian tourism minister Mamdouh El Beltagui.[6] Travel fell worldwide about 15 percent, hitting hardest those developed countries attractive to American tourists and dependent on airlines. Cruise lines reported a drop in passengers. Meetings and conferences were cancelled in great numbers, according to the World Tourism Organization, which created the Crisis Committee to meet the challenge of terrorism and restore tourist travel to its pre-attack level. For some Third World countries, tourism was the principal industry, and the assurance of safe travel had to be restored quickly. The WTO Crisis Committee gathered and shared information among its member nations.

Again, the United States had a key role in the aftermath of the infamous September attack. "The United States is essential to world tourism," stated Graham Miller of London's University of Westminster. "It generates the most amount of revenue globally."[7] To attract travelers, Mexico eliminated its sales tax on conventions and increased its advertising budget by 50 percent. Egypt committed $30 million to subsidize its air flights dependent on tourists. Because of the slump in the world economy that began in March 2001, a net measurement of the terrorist attack's impact on tourism was impossible, but mass cancellations of flights and accommodations left no doubt about its importance.

Shipping experienced only a minor setback because it had already taken some steps to dampen the effect. Some companies, especially those with elaborate pathways of supply, had made plans for the Y2K computer meltdown anticipated on January 1, 2000. Thus, procedures for moving cargoes in case of disaster were in place already for some companies. Others had taken measures to prevent robberies and hijackings. According to one spokesperson, the railroad industry had been dealing with hijackers "since the days of Jesse James."[8] Negotiations for reducing border bottlenecks were already under way between the United States and Canada. Computer tracking of freight had become a day-to-day operation for many companies.

Determining the impact of the terrorist attack on the U.S. economy could only be estimated because the business cycle was already in a downturn. For this reason wholesale inventories were high, so delays in shipping were minimal. Consumer demand had begun to fall several months prior to September 2001, and some corporations had implemented cutbacks and hiring freezes. The Wall Street bonanza of the 1990s had come to an abrupt halt in March 2001.

In October 2001, U.S. Federal Reserve Board chairman Alan Greenspan addressed the Institute for International Economics in Washington, DC. His subject was globalization and terrorism. Always a strong advocate of globalization, a concept that he admitted was "exceptionally abstract" to the general public, Greenspan emphasized that terrorism must not be allowed to shut down the avenues of trade. "More open economies have recorded the best growth performance; in contrast, countries with inward-oriented policies have done less well." He associated globalization, or the process of open and free trade, with "economic stability and political freedom." While inequities appeared, Greenspan saw the world-integrated economy as a major factor in longer life expectancies, greater social mobility, increased leisure time, and improved working conditions as well as in the ability to "enhance our environment by setting aside natural resources rather than employing them to sustain a minimum level of subsistence." In this context, he urged a forceful stance against terrorism because it "posed a challenge to the remarkable record of globalization." It was essential to ensure that the general public understood, he continued, the connection between globalization and freedom—"the antithesis of terrorism."[9]

America's global alliances underwent some realignments. President Bush formed a coalition of countries to stamp out the al-Qaeda forces and the Taliban government in Afghanistan. This so-called War on Terrorism served as the beginning of a military, economic, and diplomatic campaign expected to last several years. The World Trade Center attack depeened the longstanding alliance between London and Washington, and the United States strengthened its ties with Pakistan, India, Thailand, and South Africa. Relations with Russia improved because it wanted to see the Afghan region stabilized.

The complexity of the new global mission became apparent when a conflict developed between the military operation against al-Qaeda and the American textile industry. The United States usually imported about $2 billion worth of clothing and fabric from Pakistan each year, but importers stopped buying there because they worried about anti-American sentiment that might interrupt deliveries. For relief, Pakistan appealed to the United States to lower its tariff on textiles, but the American textile manufacturers, who had friends in Congress, opposed the request. The United States faced the dilemma of assisting its domestic industry or going to the rescue of its allies. Tariffs remained, but the White House under President Bush arranged to extend foreign aid to Pakistan.

A particularly difficult consequence of the new terrorism was its impact on the U.S. immigration policy. As intelligence agencies investigated the terrorists behind the September 11 attack, they discovered that the hijackers who piloted the airliners had learned to fly at a rudimentary level in flight schools while living in the United States. This revelation came as a shock because it was commonly assumed that the INS screened immigrants and kept out terrorists. The arrest of Ahmed Ressam in 1999 for trying to smuggle explosives across the U.S.-Canadian border now took on greater significance; he had intended to plant a carload of dynamite at Los Angeles International Airport. There was now a new sense of urgency about protecting borders, but it was accompanied by the realization that America's boundaries with Canada and Mexico were long, with vast stretches left unguarded. Certain features of globalization, particularly international air travel and the past efforts to ease traffic across borders, worsened the situation. "The sheer volume of international travel," wrote one author, "that has accompanied globalization, with more planes flying to more places and more people flying on them, has made it easier for terrorists to slip into the bigger stream."[10]

Control of the borders and enforcement of immigration rules received greater attention. Advocates such as Pat Buchanan and Peter Brimelow called for immigration reform.[11] Since the nineteen terrorists involved in the attack had links to al-Qaeda, aliens became suspect, and federal authorities launched a program, The Inititative, to arrest illegal aliens as part of a crackdown on terrorist activities. They arrested about 1,000 who were convicted felons and instigated deportation proceedings against another 314,000. The INS began checking identities of foreigners working in airports and detained anyone with false identity papers. At Salt Lake City, the site of the 2002 Winter Olympics, where extraordinary security precautions were taken, the

INS arrested several airport workers. In Florida, an effort got under way to give state officials the authority to arrest illegal aliens on civil charges.

Policing the Canadian and Mexican borders presented special problems. Traffic crossed both borders daily on a large scale, and there was a tendency for officials not to interfere or hinder the movement of innocent persons. Canada had a liberal policy toward immigrants, which made it an attractive temporary home for persons seeking to live in the United States. Migrants hoping to live in America often went there first. When Canadian officials arrested Nabil Al-Marabh, suspected of being linked to the September terrorists, for trying to enter the United States with a false passport and then released him, the different perceptions of the two countries were evident. A week later, agents of the Federal Bureau of Investigation (FBI) arrested him in Chicago. Not only people but also freight shipments were part of the flow over the borders that had to be maintained. American and Canadian authorities fought bottlenecks by instituting the "fast lane," a special clearance for carriers whose cargoes had previously been inspected at the factory or loading dock.

The history of crossings along the Mexican border, both legal and illegal, made tight security a Herculean task. National Guard troops were placed at border crossings—a move that irritated Mexico—and tighter inspection procedures at checkpoints were put into effect. Further steps for security, which likely would rely heavily on technology, would have to be agreed upon by President Bush and Mexico's President Vicente Fox.

At the six-months' observance of the September attack in March 2002, U.S. immigration legislation remained the same as before, although borders were tightened and security checks became more thorough. Military personnel were dispersed along borders in added strength. Investigations of aliens were undertaken for any possible links to al-Qaeda or other terrorist organizations. The INS came under fire for approving visas for two of the hijackers involved in the September attack six months afterward. The United States intervened in Afghanistan and overthrew the pro-terrorist Taliban government. There remained the potential for a renewed campaign to alter federal legislation on immigration. With the threat of new terrorism added to the opposition to globalization, a nationwide demand for placing restrictions on the number of immigrants allowed into the country was not impossible. Such a development, if enforced, would have an impact on Latin America, especially on Mexico, which depended on the United States to relieve the pressure of its burgeoning population, its decline in agriculture, and its worsening income inequality. If the United States shut off the "safety valve," political unrest might follow in Mexico. From this view, the new terrorism added another dimension to America's role as the leader of globalization.

NOTES

1. Paul R. Pillar, *Terrorism and U.S. Foreign Policy* (Washington, DC: Brookings Institution Press, 2001), 47.
2. *New York Times*, October 20, 2001.
3. Hans Magnus Enzenberger, "The Resurgence of Human Sacrifice," *Deutschland: Forum on Politics, Culture, Business, and Science* (October–November 2001): 13–14.
4. Benjamin R. Berber, *Jihad vs. McWorld* (New York: Times Books, 1995), 8, 205.
5. Text of President Bush's Speech, September 20, 2001, http://www.geocities.com/christymwl/USA_Bush_Speech_9-20-2001.html, p. 8, 2002.
6. http://www.hotel-online.com/Neo/News/PR2001_4th/Nov_WTOAction.html, p. 1, 2002.
7. http://secure.canoe.ca/MoneyRebuild/sept17_tourism_ap.html, p. 1. 2002.
8. *New York Times*, October 9, 2001.
9. http://uninfo.state.gov/topical/pol/terror/01102500.html, pp. 5, 7.
10. Pillar, *Terrorism and U.S. Foreign Policy*, 48.
11. See Buchanan, *The Death of the West*; and Peter Brimelow, *Alien Nation: Common Sense about America's Immigration Disaster* (New York: Random House, 1995).

8 Future Directions

The march toward globalization, beginning in 1945 and led by the United States, contributed greatly to the improved standard of living around the world and facilitated freedom of movement. In that achievement, however, real costs were incurred with the loss of jobs, damage to the environment, and the impact on cultural traditions and practices imposed by large-scale tourism and immigration. These developments set off a reaction against globalization that first appeared mostly among academics and policy analysts, which established a body of literature critical of free trade, transnational corporations, and the competitive entrepreneurial spirit associated with capitalism. In 1996 one writer asserted that globalization and the ideas it represented "have brought us to the grim situation of the moment: the spreading disintegration of the social order and the increase of poverty, landlessness, homelessness, violence, alienation, and, deep within the hearts of many people, extreme anxiety about the future."[1] So harmful were the effects of globalization, according to this assessment, that it was responsible for "climate change, ozone depletion, massive species loss, and near maximum levels of air, soil, and water pollution."[2]

The Seattle riot brought the issue of globalization to a new level, one that could now be expected to provoke strong public demonstrations and even violence. In 2001, when delegates of the Group of 8 met in Genoa, Italy, one antiglobal demonstrator died in a clash with police. Again in early 2002, demonstrators marched in New York City to protest the annual meeting of the World Economic Forum, generally known as the Davos group, of business, trade, and financial leaders. These riots and demonstrations, particularly the Seattle incident, served as a signpost in the history of globalization, marking the establishment and recognition of a strong backlash against interconnected economies and arousing fear of a return to the protectionism of the pre–World War II era.

Such bitterness and hostility rose as a counterforce to the euphoria over globalization of the previous decade. Marching into the new era of world trade had become fashionable and appeared to be synonymous with progress and modernity. The revolution in information technology, or IT, seemed to usher in a postmodern age that was hastening productivity, prosperity, and an improved standard of living. Such enthusiasm and optimism rested on the bullish economy of the 1990s, the longest-running boom since World War II. In the United States it seemed that the downturn in the business cycle, a regular feature of the American economy, had become extinct, and exuberant forecasters declared the arrival of the "New Economy." Steadily rising indexes on Wall Street and financial centers produced youthful entrepreneurs commonly known as "dot com" millionaires. In this expansive climate, the notion of borderless economies became popular, and globalization was hailed as an unfolding stage in world history.

Seattle changed this general perception of globalization. That incident, plus subsequent demonstrations, brought an unpredented awareness of the shortcomings of globalization, which turned the discussion of the subject into a two-sided argument rather than a cheerleader's yell. Protestors and critics alike pointed to the widening gap between rich and poor nations and insisted that while the practices of the world economy benefited many people, large numbers in undeveloped areas were experiencing a worsening effect. Not all participants and observers of globalization accepted that claim, but proponents of trade now had to defend themselves from dissenters.

A critical event in this development was a plunge in the world economy in 2001. In Japan, Europe, and the United States, growth slowed, stock prices plummeted, and unemployment rose. Bankruptcies multiplied among leading corporations. Hardest hit were the new technology companies, the computer and Internet startups that had worn the golden halo of the unstoppable 1990s. Dot com millionaires lost their fortunes. In this set of conditions, the aura of globalization as the driving force that pushed the world onto a new plateau of prosperity lost much of its appeal. Protests against meetings of trade leaders commanded respect, and a sense of concern over the effects of globalization started rising.

Whether it relates to trade, immigration, cultural change, technology, or other features, the interconnected world economy, however, will remain. For the United States and the major industrial powers of the world, a return to the level of international exchange of goods and services prior to World War II would be disastrous. The quality of life would drop severely without the benefits and opportunities inherent in trade. Consumers in the United States demand products made in other countries: automobiles, electronics, food, and clothing. At the same time, the United States depends on the world market to buy its goods. Regardless of how data may be interpreted, common sense shows that if we do not buy from foreign countries, we cannot sell to them. "We cannot go back on globalization," a recipient of the Nobel Prize wrote. "It is here to stay."[3]

At the start of the millennium, the world faced challenges that will require cooperation among its peoples to resolve. There remained an immediate need for research on the climate, for progress on common goals in space exploration, for improved understanding of the ecosystem and oceanography, for further research in infection biology related to new diseases, and for greater cooperation in utilizing current levels of knowledge for overcoming the traditional enemies: poverty, exploitation, disease, and ignorance. Communications technology raised the expectations of people around the world, encouraging creative impulses and fostering a young generation unwilling to be confined by national boundaries. Indeed, knowledge, or information, has become a new commodity essential for human progress, and cooperation among those institutions pursuing knowledge and higher education, business and labor organizations, human rights groups, and government-sponsored programs will only become greater. Private enterprise, with its vast financial resouces, will continue to be vital for funding research without being encumbered by the baggage of government rules and regulations. A global "knowledge society" is emerging, and cooperation will be necessary for channeling its energy into productive purposes. Those countries willing to participate in the liberal trade order will be the most innovative and will grow in the new century.[4]

For the United States, global partnerships are indispensable. Because of its high rate of consumption and a lifestyle built on the availability of resources, the country cannot afford to regress behind protective walls. Years ago the United States lost its self-sufficiency in energy, agriculture, and technology; its own domestic market cannot absorb its total production. Importing and exporting will have to continue. The same conditions apply to other developed countries.

If anything, global cooperation must increase. In developing countries where population growth, longer life expectancies, and a growing middle class push rates of consumption higher, there is a need for more food, shelter, medical care, education, and other essentials. World productivity must increase to feed more mouths and growing consumer appetites. Poor countries already clamor for more goods and services. India and China, two countries known for their poverty and rejection of international trade, had by the 1990s begun to seek partners in the world market, and by the twenty-first century they were emerging as major players in international trade.[5]

New markets will open as the states of the former Soviet Union seek to modernize their economies. Admittedly the investor rush into Russia upon the collapse of the Communist regime in 1991 did not produce the anticipated results, but there remains much potential. A similar pattern is found with the former satellite countries, but political issues and the lack of a financial structure for private operations doomed those early efforts. In 2002, China offered potential as a new market. Its membership in the World Trade Organization, which became effective in 2002, stirred considerable enthusiasm among transnational corporations and various investors for trade there. In 1996 the Coca-Cola Bottling Company sold 3 billion Cokes in China. There are similar expectations in regard to Latin America, where the fever of trade has been caught. Mexico's partnership with NAFTA and the four-nation MERCOSUR trade agreement—involving Argentina, Brazil, Paraguay, and Uruguay—aroused much anticipation of an expanding economy. The enthusiasm for regional trade agreements in Asia, Latin America, and Europe indicated a desire to join the movement toward globalization. Adoption by the European Union (EU) of the euro, which went into circulation in 2002, was further evidence that efficiency and convenience can be enhanced through unified action. Admittedly the major blocs—WTO, NAFTA, and EU—grew during the prosperous 1990s and would have to prove their mettle with the global economic downturn starting in 2001.

The rise of the new terrorism, which erupted like a volcano in September 2001, put globalization onto another plateau. With the onset of fanatical, suicidal Islamic terrorists who oppose globalization, the major trading nations of the world now have a common enemy that bind them together for reasons not related to economics. Nations cannot shut themselves off from the threat because today's terrorists operate like a transnational corporation, though clandestinely. For their own security, nations must rely on the tools of global trade such as information technology, and they must cooperate in pooling their resources, particularly intelligence. For those nations eagerly stepping forward into modernity, today's faceless terrorism requires them to protect each other as would a band of warriors surrounded by a barbaric and ruthless enemy.

With the defeat of fascism and militarism in World War II and the collapse of the Soviet Communist regime, capitalism triumphed. History left the United States as the sole superpower in 2002, with the world's advanced industrial nations as allies. America's military supremacy and economic strength gave it a leadership role which it could not refuse. It had taken this role in 1945, and at the beginning of the twenty-first century it employed the same combination of military action and world trade used then. The rhetoric used to rally the nation to arms and to the commitment to a long war against terrorism, reinforced by a surge of patriotism, renewed the country's leadership position. A sense of mission gripped the nation as it saw a threat to civilization, and it could be expected to maintain vigilance against terrorism. The importance of allies became clear again, indicating that coalition leadership would be needed once more as the United States served as policeman to the world.

Because of the ruthless nature of capitalism to heap rewards on some people while ignoring others—a process inherent in global trade—inequities of globalization will continue and thereby cause unrest. Analysts commonly warn that ways must be found to bring help to those people not benefiting from the integrated world economy. Herein lies the greatest danger. For its own self-interests as well as for humanitarianism, the United States along with its closest allies should probe for new pathways to extend globalization's benefits to more people. This effort may focus on the growing income gaps within trading partners as well as on whole countries left behind by globalization. Responsibility will bear upon American policymakers to formulate trade policies so as to include opportunities for the poor and dispossessed. The rising middle class in Third World countries must also be brought into the circle, for from within that group, aspiring to achieve social mobility, will come the leadership for both positive and negative forces.

Demands for protectionism will continue. Even among advocates of trade, disagreements erupt over the imposition of temporary tariffs to protect businesses and jobs from "dumping" by international competitors. Within trade organizations such as the WTO there are provisions for blocking imports. Steel and textiles are two American industries that constantly face import threats, and their leaders in both cases appeal to Congress and the White House for relief. Depending on the merits of the appeals, and the political fallout, restrictions may be imposed. Other countries exercising their WTO rights may ask for arbitration, usually a slow and cumbersome process, and they may resort to retribution that could set off a trade war. Appeals come before the world's various trade organizations at a steady rate, and they are often resolved through natural market forces rather than arbitration tribunals. Hardly any country escapes injury-free from international trade, however, despite the efforts to prevent unfair practices.

Within the United States the ebb and flow of protectionism usually paralleled the condition of the economy. Calls for restriction generally followed downturns in the business cycle and in employment. Certain special interests, particularly labor unions, made the loudest demands for protectionism on the grounds that open trade benefited businesses at the expense of workers. In 2002 the United States slapped a temporary tariff on foreign steel for these reasons. The decision was controversial and the subject of much discussion among policymakers and the media. Invariably the decisions over tariff duties become embroiled in domestic politics, which keeps trade policy in the public eye.

The clamor against globalization often becomes emotional, including an attack upon the presumption that free trade improves economic conditions. Free trade, critics allege, brought a loss of jobs because it placed American manufacturing firms at a competitive disadvantage with foreign companies having lower operating costs, especially lower wages. In the United States this issue surfaced repeatedly during congressional debates over trade policy and reached a high pitch during the 1992 presidential election when Reform Party candidate Ross Perot urged that the United States not ratify the accord letting Mexico join NAFTA. Powerful political forces echoed Perot's cry, including liberal Democratic senator Richard Gephardt and conservative spokesperson Pat Buchanan. Union leaders were among the harshest critics of free trade.

Whenever an American consumer purchased an import such as a Japanese automobile, so opponents argued, it meant the lost sale of an American vehicle. When a large-enough number of foreign-made automobiles sold in the domestic market, the total had an impact on U.S.

manufacturers, who then would have to lower their production forecasts and lay off workers. By taking into account the large influx of imported goods such as electronics, appliances, and numerous other items besides automobiles, the impact of open trading had repercussions for the U.S. economy. Critics legitimately pointed to the decline of manufacturing in the United States in the last quarter-century and used it as proof of their argument. Wages also fell among workers in manufacturing because they had to compete with unskilled workers in foreign companies. If purchasing power declined far enough, consumers would have to resort to buying lower-priced imported goods. This development would allegedly injure the U.S. economy because the country would be unable to defend itself from foreign competition.

For evidence, critics cited the fact that job losses occurred in textiles, furniture manufacturing, garment making, and electronics assembly. Employment in the unskilled sector of manufacturing did fall in the 1990s, partly due to the importation of cheaper goods and the relocation of factories and plants across borders. Manufacturing employment in the 1990s compared poorly with the 1950s. It supported one-third of U.S. wage-earner jobs in 1950, but only one-seventh in the 1990s.[6] A decline in the relative importance of manufacturing as a supplier of jobs had indeed taken place, seemingly reinforcing the claim that free trade, the key to globalization, hurt the economy.

Defenders of free trade acknowledged the relative decline of manufacturing, but they insisted that a more thorough analysis and investigation of the issue changed the context. To begin with, one study claimed that the total number of workers in manufacturing actually increased, but the growth of other industries, especially service, grew faster and pushed down manufacturing's rank as an employer. Losses within steel dramatized the negative aspect of open trade, but defenders remained convinced that the overall increase in jobs in other sectors offset the losses. Heavy industries such as steel received a smaller portion of the consumers' dollar because as the U.S. standard of living rose in the last half-century, consumers spent relatively less on manufactured goods and more on services. Throughout the period of free trade, total employment rose, thus encouraging economists of liberal trade to conclude that improvements in employment paralleled the growth of international trade.

A major repercussion of globalization was, however, the declining political strength of traditional protectionist interests. Unions, once a powerful lobby in American politics, have experienced a steady decline in membership and political clout. Transnational corporations competing on a global scale sometimes moved their operations into low-wage countries, causing a loss of jobs, but the ability of foreign competitors to manufacture some items more efficiently took over a portion of the international market share. Traditional blue-collar, low-skilled jobs shrank. The expansion of the service sector also meant that new jobs were created in professions usually not affiliated with unions. Technology, particularly in information services, accounted for much of the change.

Other factors explained the drop in union strength: deregulation, privatization, and the increasing reluctance by employees to remain with one company or industry over time. The growing difficulty of large corporations in maintaining generous retirement programs also reduced the workers' loyalty to a single firm. Job or career change became more common in the U.S. workforce. Hence, a combination of circumstances explained the changing dynamics responsible for the decline of protectionism.

Free traders believe, of course, that trade creates more jobs than it loses, although they acknowledge that low-skilled workers are usually hit the worst. Certainly, arguments arise over the data supporting or challenging this claim. Advocates of open trade feel compelled to maintain a constant watch over trade policy, fearing a resurgence of protectionist strength. "Like Dracula, protectionism never really dies," wrote one official, "and we who support free trade must always keep our intellectual wooden stakes sharp and ready."[7]

To maintain its standard of living and its lifestyle of exorbitance, the United States must remain competitive in the world market. Research and technological development have particular importance since U.S. industries compete with many low-wage countries whose industries are comparatively unfettered by environmental regulations. American agriculture encountered this condition soon after the end of World War II, but mechanization and the practice of high-yield cultivation kept agriculture a viable part of the U.S. economy. Loss of its labor supply to urbanization also pushed the drive toward mechanization. Despite its progress toward modernization, however, agriculture remained dependent on government subsidies.

For the first generation after World War II, American industry faced comparatively little competition as it enjoyed a booming domestic and overseas demand for its products. By the 1970s, Europe and Japan had overcome the wartime devastation to their economies, which accounted for their modern and efficient methods of production. The new technologies of information were easily accessible to them, too, so that America's heavy industries went through a period of decline and caused the northeastern U.S. manufacturing region to be known as the Rust Belt. By modernizing and shifting to newer products and markets, the area began to revive in the 1990s.

Modifications of immigration policy may occur, but they will be a consequence of the concern over terrorism rather than an effort to curb the effects of globalization. Recommendations for preserving racial balances or cultural characteristics will not succeed, but a call for the sake of security may stir action. As long as the economies of Latin America, and particularly Mexico, cannot absorb their displaced agricultural workers, migration across the southern borders into the United States will continue. Only if employment opportunities decline for them in this country will these migrants be prone to stay at home. A small percentage of those already here may choose in that case to return to their native land, but without a major economic setback in the United States, the demographic composition of states bordering Mexico should be expected to continue becoming more Hispanic. Within a generation the general population in those states could be 50 percent Latino. Security measures alone cannot stop the migration.

Trade, along with various forms of foreign aid, will continue to be regarded as the most opportunistic means for improving the standard of living in the Third World. Factors such as corruption, poorly administered rules of law, and political elitism may receive new emphasis in the efforts to uplift the quality of life around the world, but American policymakers, holding offers of support, will likely frown upon the implementation of any severe protectionist barriers by a recipient of U.S. aid. Global lenders such as the IMF and the World Bank will continue to demand that governments install Keynesian measures to regulate their monetary practices and provide social protection. The United States will remain the principal player in the efforts to direct and promote the integrated world economy. One poll taken in 2000 showed that "Americans are broadly in favor of globalization."[8]

Technology will continue to exert a strong influence on economic and cultural affairs, with the most immediate impact occurring in the poorer countries where it is left undeveloped. There remain many areas of the world where current technologies could be put to use if the infrastructure and other supporting factors required for them were available, particularly in parts of Africa, Asia, and Latin America. In order to become part of the "knowledge society," the developing countries will seek to promote their communications systems, which will encourage them to search for capital. Lending institutions such as the World Bank will be expected to supply capital. Restrictions on information may increase as concerns grow over property rights and privacy issues in the developed nations.

Entrepreneurship will also continue to be important because transnational corporations remain the basic instrument through which new technologies and other benefits of modernity become available. Within those organizations must come the managerial skills and abilities to conduct business at an international level. Even as governments strive to promote labor rights and protection of the environment, they will continue to seek transnationals as partners because of their experience and expertise in world business affairs.

Disagreements over labor, the environment, and international lending institutions led to the greatest challenge thrown at globalization: that the nature of the new interconnected world economy caused it to encroach upon the sovereignty of governments and threatened democracy. Some of America's most popular spokespersons for economic and social justice held this view and warned that adjustments and corrections must be made to protect the rights of citizens from the effects of globalization. Warnings about the loss of sovereignty nearly always focused on the authority and power given away to trade organizations by governments when they ratify an agreement. Multinational corporations received the blame for this development as behind-the-scenes manipulators and lobbyists that managed to get trade alignments structured for their benefit. Ralph Nader and co-author Lori Wallach claimed, for example, that agreements such as the WTO and NAFTA place "every government in a virtual hostage situation, at the mercy of a global financial and commercial system run by empowered corporations."[9] In 1998, Pat Buchanan published *The Great Betrayal*, warning: "We do not need to trade away our sovereignty for a seat at the table of some global regime."[10] Some writers, when analyzing the characteristics of global economics, predicted that "borderless societies" would replace the standard territorial countries, which would limit their "ability both to confine the effects of domestic economic policy within national borders and to insulate countries from foreign economic shocks."[11] As stated by one analyst, "Transnational corporations will have the World Trade Organization's legal powers to overrule the existing laws of countries at all levels."[12]

Among the potentially more damaging aspects of the threat to national sovereignty, one involved provisions in international trade organizations known as "multilateral agreements on investment." It pertains to the rights and provisions given to foreign investors as they employ workers, rely on the infrastructure, use environmental resources, and the like. The best-known example is Chapter 11 in the NAFTA accord, which attempts to ensure that foreign investors will not face unfair treatment from host governments. According to NAFTA, such investors are entitled to the same procedures of due process as local and domestic companies. Chapter 11 heightens the controversy over sovereignty when disputes occur, which happened in a case in which a NAFTA tribunal made a final decision that overrode the state law in the United States.

The case of *Loewen Group, Inc. vs. United States*, adjudicated in 2001, became the subject of a television documentary. In an appeal from the Canadian firm Loewen Group, a NAFTA tribunal reversed a multimillion-dollar judgment against Loewen by a Mississippi jury and ordered the U.S. government to compensate the Canadian firm. Critics of globalization viewed this case as an example of NAFTA's potential threat to the judicial system of the United States, a fundamental pillar of American democracy. Since the NAFTA reversal, business interests along with citizens' groups have begun to lobby Congress for legislation to prevent abuses of state laws. Incidents such as the Loewen case drove the apprehension and concern over the loss of sovereignty to a higher level, and in 2001 a special panel of the United Nations addressed this question. It acknowledged that new "emerging political, economic, social, and cultural challenges" required the role of government to be redefined, but with no implication of a loss of sovereignty.[13]

Owing to the new practices in banking and investment wrought by technology, the UN panel recommended that governments reconfigure their monetary policies so as to ensure sufficient capital for social needs as well as trade. Recognizing that Third World countries had the greatest difficulty in coping with the effects of globalization, the panel urged them—particularly African countries—to take a variety of steps addressing their own institutions, such as improving administration and providing social protection. The conclusion of the panel agreed with most scholars and analysts examining the relationship of government to globalization. They commonly recommended more government action, believing that the state will continue to thrive but that it may have to forfeit some traditional activities and accept new responsibilities. One of the most insightful observations on the role of government in the context of globalization had come in 2000 from the United Nations Development Program. Bad government, meaning inefficient administration, corruption, and lack of forceful leadership in providing social programs, was responsible for much of the poverty in the Third World.[14]

While critics claimed governments were losing sovereignty, a broad-based demand for greater government intervention was already under way. There was a growing conviction that adjustments in trade policy were necessary. International trade improved the incomes of those people able to tap into the economic activity associated with it, but segments of the world population, including the United States, failed to reap the opportunities, thus causing income inequality to worsen. This effect of globalization had become more widely recognized. As recommended by one writer, a return to protectionism should be avoided, but "policy makers ought instead to complement the external strategy of liberalization with an internal strategy of compensation, training, and social insurance for those groups who are most at risk."[15]

This daunting task will reassert the authority of government and leave the question of sovereignty on the bookshelves. Each trading partner should be expected, however, to protect its own interests even while it remains a cooperative member of trade agreements. For that reason, arbitration will continue to be used for reconciliation of trade disputes because member nations of agreements will be forced to stand together for economic strength and protection from outside threats such as terrorism. The instruments of globalization—the International Monetary Fund, the World Bank, NAFTA, the WTO, and the United Nations—will continue to hold their positions of prominence and authority despite their critics because of the importance of arbitration of disputes and because of the growing realization that trade policies have ethical dimensions.

Within the framework of the rising expectations of Third World peoples, emerging new technologies, and the birth and death of regimes, all of which challenge orthodoxy, free trade popularly persisted as the practice most likely to improve the lives of the impoverished around the world. Adjustments in the role of government seemed likely, but each U.S. president since 1945 touted trade as the best policy among the alternatives for promoting peace and security. In 2000, when President Bill Clinton urged the World Economic Forum of business leaders in Davos, Switzerland, to listen to the critics and take into consideration their pleas for labor rights and environmental protection, he nonetheless endorsed world trade. In 2001 his successor, President George W. Bush, told the Organization of American States that "open trade fuels the engine of economic growth that creates the new jobs and new income," and Federal Reserve Board chairman Alan Greenspan insisted in 2000 that globalization improved conditions within countries participating in international trade.[16] None veered from President Harry Truman's call in 1945 for the United States to exert leadership in improving the world economy.

Within the new millennium, globalization had reached a new stage, passing the "internationalization" of the late nineteenth century and becoming well entrenched through various new technologies, trade agreements, and national policies. Its shortcomings had burst onto the international scene through riots and demonstrations and forced themselves upon world leaders; issues involving the fundamental rights of humanity could no longer be ignored. Globalization had gone beyond its original definition as expressed in economic terms and had come to be recognized in humanistic terms, encompassing the movement of people across borders, the spreading of cultures, and the threats to public health. Globalization had acquired an ethical dimension, according to the United Nations, and had to be guided by "principles of ethics and democracy . . . based on the understanding that it is necessary to follow a course that leads to worldwide progress seen as human development."[17]

Looking back over the last fifty years, the United States took the leading role in promoting trade. Chiefly by means of the Cold War, trade agreements, and technological development, it became a hegemonic power, but as the forces of globalization matured, the United States also got caught in its sweeping power. America will be expected to furnish leadership because a downturn in its economy affects much of the world; it will continue to be regarded as the international engine of growth.

Only recently has the impact of globalization become apparent in the United States and received recognition. In the broad sweep of history over the last half-century, the decline of communism, the end of imperialism, the emergence of the knowledge society, the rising expectations of people around the world, large-scale migration, the resurgence of infectious diseases, the rise of transnational corporations, global trade agreements, and the impact of technology all came together to produce the integrated world economy. In 1945 the United States did not anticipate such a development, but its commitment to redirecting the world economy away from the restrictionist culture and practices of the previous generation set the country on the path to globalization.

Since 1945 the United States has had a strong economy and a rising standard of living, though income inequalities and poverty persisted. It managed to extend foreign aid for various reasons, including self-interest, but it nonetheless shunted capital and resources around the world. The American economy also attracted capital from foreign investors, an indication of the world's trust in the economy, a practice that continued at the end of the twentieth century. This condition kept the United States as the financial center of the global economy and portended the leading role for the country in the future growth of the integrated world economy.

The ability of the United States to attract foreign capital as well as millions of people seeking a new life rested on the reliability of its economy, ranging from the soundness of the dollar to the assurance that trade agreements and contracts would be honored. It also rested on the political stability of the country and the spirit of freedom and opportunity inherent in the system of governance and equal protection of the law. In these respects the United States has not been flawless, and it appeared to be in need of a reevaluation of certain aspects of its lifestyle, but it remained a popular destination for millions of people and the expected role leader in global development.

In the past, trade meant the exchange of products ranging from raw agricultural commodities to high-tech manufactured computer chips. Ships laden with cotton bales, logs, iron ore, automobiles, electrical appliances, clothing or even crude oil steamed from port to port with their valuable cargoes destined for homes, factories, and farms. As the world becomes increasingly global, however, trade will become more broadly defined and more complex, and it will involve items of value not exchanged on the world market in the past. Already, currency flows across borders sometimes ruthlessly. With technological advances in medicine, it is conceivable that body parts—hearts, kidneys, or limbs—could readily flow under highly supervised care. Transnationals may trade labor, exchanging the time of highly skilled employees for other skills needed for particular jobs. Human rights would have to be protected, of course, but while the transfer of employees within corporations is common practice, companies may arrange to exchange employees on a basis similar to the routine of sports teams trading players. Highly prized research information and data could be bought and sold in a manner similar to stocks. Small but well-equipped and highly trained military and security units employed for public or private safety may be an item of trade if terrorism spreads. Under such imposing conditions, prosperity, or even safety, will depend on the ability to raise capital, organize, communicate, and successfully execute operations on a global scale.

Despite the rise of multinational corporations, technology will encourage individualism among the highly skilled and alter their career paths. With the use of information technology, a trend is under way for individual entrepreneurs to work in their homes on a contract basis with large firms and enjoy more flexible working hours and freedom of travel. Wishing to avoid the cost and liability of employing full-time workers, companies will pursue people with talent who can perform particular tasks as self-employed individuals. Both workers and companies will have greater flexibility and be free to pursue creative ideas and experiment with unorthodox proposals. Such self-employed and talented persons will not have the usual work schedules, nor will they spend their careers with only one firm. The relationship will be less along the traditional line of worker-management but closer to corporation–venture capitalist. For this segment of the workforce, a lifestyle based on flexibility and independence will become more common.

Globalization will advance and retreat depending on the state of the world economy, but political factors will also have an impact on the relationship of trading nations and the ability of the poor and aspiring nations to tap into the integrated world economy. As our understanding and knowledge of the interconnected world grows, it becomes apparent that globalization transcends economics and includes the movement of people, human rights, ethical considerations, and freedom of choice. These considerations guided the United States when it entered World War II over one-half century ago, and they remain its guiding principles as a world leader.

NOTES

1. Mander, "Facing the Rising Tide," 3–4.
2. Ibid.
3. Joseph E. Stiglitz, "Globalizaton and Its Discontents," *Deutschland* (August–September 2002): 11.
4. Hubert Markl, "Competition for the Best Ideas," *Deutschland* (April–May 2001): 3.
5. Daniel Yergin and Joseph Stanislaw, *The Commanding Heights: The Battle for the World Economy*, 185–230.
6. Burtless et al., *Globaphobia*, 51–52.
7. Bob McTeer, "Economic Protectionism," *Economic Insights* 6, no. 2 (Dallas: Federal Reserve System, 2001).
8. *The Economist* (September 30, 2000): 8.
9. Ralph Nader and Lori Wallach, "GATT, NAFTA, and the Subversion of the Democratic Process," in *The Case against the Global Economy and for a Turn toward the Local*, ed. Jerry Mander and Edward Goldsmith (San Francisco: Sierra Club Books, 1996), 93.
10. Patrick J. Buchanan, *The Great Betrayal: How American Sovereignty and Social Justice Are Being Sacrificed to the Gods of the Global Economy* (Boston: Little, Brown and Company, 1998), 74.
11. Janet Ceglowski, "Has Globalization Created a Borderless World?" in *Globalization and the Challenges of a New Century*, ed. Patrick O'Meara, Howard D. Mehlinger, and Matthew Krain (Bloomington: Indiana University Press, 2000), 101.
12. Trade Fast Track Agreements, http://www.udarrell.com/fasttrack.html, p. 1, 2002.
13. Globalization Panel, http://www.unpan1.un.org/intrades/groups/public/documents/un/unpan001917.pdf, 2002.
14. *New York Times*, April 5, 2000.
15. Dani Rodrik, "Sense and Nonsense in the Globalization Debate," in *Globalization and the Challenges of a New Century*, ed. Patrick O'Meara, Howard D. Mehlinger, and Matthew Krain (Bloomington: Indiana University Press, 2000), 238.
16. *Dallas Morning News*, January 30, 2000; quote in http://www.issues2000.org/Celeb/George_W_Bush_Free_Trade.html, p. 2, 2002; *New York Times*, November 15, 2000.
17. Globalization Panel, http://www.unpan1.un.org/intradoc/groups/public/documents/un/unpan001917.pdf, 2002.

BIBLIOGRAPHY

Books

Allison, Gary D. *Japan's Postwar History.* Ithaca, NY: Cornell University Press, 1997.

Altbach, Philip G. *Comparative Higher Education: Knowledge, the University, and Development.* Greenwich, CT: Ablex, 1998.

Ambrose, Stephen. *Rise to Globalism: American Foreign Policy since 1938.* 6th rev. ed. New York: Penguin Books, 1991.

Anderson, Sarah, John Cavanaugh, Thea Lea, and the Institute for Policy Studies. *Field Guide to the Global Economy.* New York: The New Press, 2000.

Barnet, Richard J., and Ronald E. Muller. *Global Reach: The Power of the Multinational Corporations.* New York: Simon and Schuster, 1974.

Becker, William H., and Samuel F. Wells Jr. *Economics and World Power: An Assessment of American Diplomacy since 1789.* New York: Columbia University Press, 1984.

Berber, Benjamin R. *Jihad vs. McWorld.* New York: Times Books, 1995.

Buchanan, Patrick J. *The Death of the West: How Dying Populations and Immigrant Invasions Imperil Our Country and Civilization.* New York: Thomas Dunne Books, 2002.

_____. *The Great Betrayal: How American Sovereignty and Social Justice Are Being Sacrificed to the Gods of the Global Economy.* Boston: Little, Brown and Company, 1998.

Burnett, Robert. *The Global Jukebox: The International Music Industry.* London: Routledge, 1996.

Burtless, Gary, Robert Z. Lawrence, Robert E. Litan, and Robert J. Shapiro. *Globaphobia: Confronting Fears about Open Trade.* Washington, DC: Brookings Institution Press, 1998.

Carbaugh, Robert J. *International Economics.* 7th ed. Cincinnati: South-Western College Publishing, 2000.

Castells, Manuel. *The Rise of the Network Society*, Vol. 1 of *The Information Age: Economy, Society and Culture*. Oxford, Eng.: Blackwell, 1996.

Coerver, Donald, and Linda B. Hall. *Tangled Destinies: Latin America and the United States*. Albuquerque: University of New Mexico Press, 1999.

Crystal, David. *English as a Global Language*. Cambridge, Eng.: Cambridge University Press, 1997.

Daniels, Roger. *American Immigration: A Student Companion*. Oxford, Eng.: Oxford University Press, 2001.

De Kadt, Emanuel. *Tourism: Passport to Development? Perspectives on the Social and Cultural Effects of Tourism in Developing Countries*. New York: Oxford University Press, 1979.

Dicken, Peter. *Global Shift: Transforming the World Economy*. New York: Guilford Press, 1998.

Dickerson, Kitty G. *Textiles and Apparel in the Global Economy*. 2d ed. Englewood Cliffs, NJ: Prentice-Hall, 1995.

_____. *Textiles and Apparel in the Global Economy*. 3d ed. Upper Saddle River, NJ: Merrill, 1999.

Divine, Robert A. *Second Chance: The Triumph of Internationalism in America during World War II*. New York: Atheneum, 1967.

Dukes, Paul. *The Superpowers: A Short History*. London: Routledge, 2000.

Faulkner, Harold U. *American Economic History*. 8th ed. New York: Harper and Brothers, 1960.

Friedman, Thomas L. *The Lexus and the Olive Tree*. New York: Anchor Books, 2000.

Gore, Al. *Earth in the Balance: Ecology and the Human Spirit*. Boston: Houghton Mifflin and Company, 1992.

Hammond, Allen. *Which World? Scenarios for the 21st Century: Global Destinies, Regional Choices*. Washington, DC: Island Press, 2000.

Harrison, David, ed. *Tourism and the Less Developed Countries*. New York: Halsted Press, 1992.

Hook, Steven W., and John Spanier. *American Foreign Policy since World War II*. 15th ed. Washington, DC: CQ Press, 2000.

Inayatullah, Sohail, and Jennifer Gidley. *The University in Transformation: Global Perspectives on the Futures of the University*. Westport, CT: Bergin and Garvey, 2000.

Johnston, R. J., Peter J. Taylor, and Michael J. Watts, eds. *Geographies of Global Change: Remapping the World in the Late Twentieth Century*. Oxford, Eng.: Blackwell, 1996.

Karantnycky, Adrian. *Jihad: The Rise of Militant Islam in Central Asia*. New Haven: Yale University Press, 2002.

Kemp, Tom. *The Climax of Capitalism: The U.S. Economy in the Twentieth Century*. London: Longman's, 1990.

Kennedy, David M. *Freedom from Fear: The American People in Depression and War, 1929–1945*. New York: Oxford University Press, 1999.

Kepel, Gilles. *Jihad: The Trail of Political Islam*. Boston: Harvard University Press, 2002.

Kunz, Diane B. *Butter and Guns: America's Cold War Economic Diplomacy*. New York: Free Press, 1997.

LaFeber, Walter. *Michael Jordan and the New Global Capitalism*. New York: W. W. Norton, 1999.

Laver, Murray. *Information Technology: Agent of Change.* Cambridge, Eng.: Cambridge University Press, 1989.

MacLachlan, Colin M., and William H. Beezley. *El Gran Pueblo: A Study of Greater Mexico.* 2d ed. Upper Saddle River, NJ: Prentice-Hall, 1999.

Mander, Jerry, and Edward Goldsmith, eds. *The Case against the Global Economy and for a Turn toward the Local.* San Francisco: Sierra Club Books, 1996.

McCullough, David. *Truman.* New York: Simon and Schuster, 1992; Touchstone Books, 1993.

McDougal, Walter A. *Promised Land, Crusader State: The American Encounter with the World since 1776.* Boston: Houghton Mifflin, 1997.

McNeill, J. R. *An Environmental History of the Twentieth Century World: Something New under the Sun.* New York: W. W. Norton, 2000.

Micklethwait, John, and Adrian Wooldridge. *A Future Perfect: The Essentials of Globalization.* New York: Crown, 2000.

Mieczkowski, Zbigniew. *World Trends in Tourism and Recreation.* New York: Peter Lang, 1990.

Morley, David. *Television, Audiences, and Cultural Studies.* London: Routledge, 1992.

Mundo, Philip A. *National Politics in a Global Economy: The Domestic Sources of U.S. Trade Policy.* Washington, DC: Georgetown University Press, 1999.

Pells, Richard. *Not Like Us: How Europeans Have Loved, Hated, and Transformed American Culture since World War II.* New York: Basic Books, 1997.

Pillar, Paul R. *Terrorism and U.S. Foreign Policy.* Washington, DC: Brookings Institution Press, 2001.

Rodrik, Dani. *Has Globalization Gone Too Far?* Washington, DC: Institute for International Economics, 1997.

Standard & Poor's. *Industry Surveys: Autos and Auto Parts.* New York: McGraw-Hill, June 14, 2001.

Steel, Ronald. *Pax Americana.* New York: Viking Press, 1967.

Stromquist, Nelly P., and Karen Monkman. *Globalization and Education: Integration and Contestation across Cultures.* Lanham, MD: Rowman and Littlefield, 2000.

Suro, Robert. *Watching America's Door: The Immigrant Backlash and the New Policy Debate.* New York: The Twentieth Century Fund Press, 1996.

Tardiff, Joseph C., ed. *U.S. Industry Profiles: The Leading 100.* Detroit: Gale, 1998.

Theobald, William, ed. *Global Tourism: The Next Decade.* Oxford, Eng.: Butterworth-Heinemann, 1995.

Tomlinson, John. *Globalization and Culture.* Chicago: University of Chicago Press, 1999.

U.S. Census Bureau. *Statistical Abstract of the United States, 2000.* 120th ed. Washington, DC, 2000.

Yergin, Daniel, and Joseph Stanislaw. *The Commanding Heights: The Battle between Government and the Marketplace That Is Remaking the Modern World.* New York. Simon and Schuster, 1998.

_____. *The Commanding Heights: The Battle for the World Economy.* New York: Simon and Schuster, 1998; Touchstone Books, 2002.

Zachary, G. Pascal. *Global Me: New Cosmopolitans and the Competitive Edge, Picking Winners and Losers.* New York: Public Affairs, 2000.

Articles and Chapters

Bade, Klaus J. "The German Hub: Migration in History and the Present," *Deutschland* 6 (December 1999–January 2000): 38–43.

Brown, D. Clayton. "The International Institute for Cotton: The Globalization of Cotton since 1945," *Agricultural History* 74 (Spring 2000): 258–71.

Ceglowski, Janet. "Has Globalization Created a Borderless World?" In *Globalization and the Challenges of a New Century*, ed. Patrick O'Meara, Howard D. Mehlinger, and Matthew Krain. Bloomington: Indiana University Press, 2000.

Clark, Tony. "Mechanisms of Corporate Rule." In *The Case against the Global Economy and for a Turn toward the Local*, ed. Jerry Mander and Edward Goldsmith. San Francisco: Sierra Club Books, 1996.

Daniels, Roger. "Changes in Immigration Law and Nativism since 1924." In *The History of Immigration of Asian Americans*, ed. Franklin Ng. New York: Garland, 1998.

Goldsmith, Edward. "Global Trade and the Environment." In *The Case against the Global Economy and for a Turn toward the Local*, ed. Jerry Mander and Edward Goldsmith. San Francisco: Sierra Club Books, 1996.

Horberg-Hodge, Helena. "Shifting Directions: From Global Dependence to Local Interdependence." In *The Case against the Global Economy and for a Turn toward the Local*, ed. Jerry Mander and Edward Goldsmith. San Francisco: Sierra Club Books, 1996.

Kravis, Irving B. "The U.S. Common Position and the Common Market." In *The Common Market: Progress and Controversy*, ed. Lawrence B. Krause. Englewood Cliffs, NJ: Prentice-Hall, 1964.

Mander, Jerry. "Facing the Rising Tide." In *The Case against the Global Economy and for a Turn toward the Local*, ed. Jerry Mander and Edward Goldsmith. San Francisco: Sierra Club Books, 1996.

Markl, Hubert. "Competition for the Best Ideas," *Deutschland* (April–May 2001): 3.

McTeer, Bob. "Economic Protectionism," *Economic Insights* 6, no. 2 (Dallas: Federal Reserve System, 2001): 1–4.

Nader, Ralph, and Lori Wallach. "GATT, NAFTA, and the Subversion of the Democratic Process." In *The Case against the Global Economy and for a Turn toward the Local*, ed. Jerry Mander and Edward Goldsmith. San Francisco: Sierra Club Books, 1996.

Rodrik, Dani. "Sense and Nonsense in the Globalization Debate." In *Globalization and the Challenges of a New Century*, ed. Patrick O'Meara, Howard D. Mehlinger, and Matthew Krain. Bloomington: Indiana University Press, 2000.

Schluter, Regina G. "Tourism Development: A Latin American Perspective." In *Global Tourism: The Next Decade*, ed. William Theobald. Oxford, Eng.: Butterworth-Heinemann, 1995.

Sims, Melvin E. "U.S. Marketing Practices around the World." In U.S. Department of Agriculture, *U.S. Agriculture in a Global Economy: 1985 Yearbook of Agriculture*. Washington, DC, 1985.

Sobel, Jeffrey. "Food System Globalization: Eating Transformations and Nutrition Transitions." In *Food in Global History*, ed. Raymond Grew. Boulder, CO: Westview Press, 1999.

Stiglitz, Joseph E. "Globalization and Its Discontents," *Deutschland* (August–September 2002): 11.

Vellas, François. "Strategic Marketing in the Air Transport Sector." In *The International Marketing of Travel and Tourism: A Strategic Approach*, ed. François Vellas and Lionel Becherel. New York: St. Martin's Press, 1999.

Zachary, G. Pascal. "New Cosmopolitans," *Deutschland* 6 (December 1999–January 2000): 64.

Periodicals

The Economist, 1981–2002; esp. March 25, September 30, 2000; August 11, 2001; September 14, November 2, 2002.

Loveland (Colorado) *Daily Report-Herald*, August 11, 2001.

Newsweek, August 27, 2001.

New York Times, 1945–2002; esp. October 30, 1998; December 2, 1999; April 5, 17, July 20, September 3, December 18, 2000; May 8, October 9, 20, 2001; February 2, 9, April 7, September 7, 2002.

Progressive Farmer, September 2001.

San Francisco Chronicle, January 6, 2002.

Internet Sites

Big Mac Currencies. http://www.economist.com/markets/bigmac/displaystory.cfm?story_id=305167. 2002.

Crisis Committee of the World Tourism Organization. http://www.hotel-online.com/Neo/News/PR2001_4thNov01_WTOAction.html. 2002.

Diseases. http://www.hopkins-id.edu/diseases/tb_epi.html. 2002.

Federal Reserve's Greenspan on Globalization, Terrorism. http://usinfo.state.gov/topical/pol/terror/01102500.html. 2002.

General Assembly Unifies Global Tourism Industry in Crisis. http://www.world-tourism.org/newsroom/Releases/more_releases/gadaily06.htm. 2002.

Immigration and Naturalization Service. http://www.ins.usdoj.gov/graphics/aboutins/statistics/299.htm. 2002

Immigration and Poverty. http://www.fairus.org//html/04169910.html. 2002.

Issues 2001. http://www.issues200.org/Celeb/George_W_Bush_Environment.htm. 2002.

Issues 2001. http://www.issues2000.org/Celeb/George_W_Bush_Immigration.htm. 2002.

Issues 2001. http://www.issues2000.org/Celeb/Al_Gore_Immigration.htm.. 2002.

Issues 2001. http://www.issues2000.org/Celeb/Al_Gore_Environment.htm.. 2002.

MEChA Calls for the Liberation of Aztlan. http://www.americanpatrol.com/MECHA/AZTLAN.html. 2002.

Mobilization for Global Justice. http://www.a16.org. 2002.

NAFTA Impact on Agriculture. http://www.ers.usda.gov/briefing/NAFTA/impact.htm. 2002.

North American Integration and Development Center. http://naid.sppsr.ucla.edu. 2002.

Original quote appeared in *San Francisco Examiner*, October 27, 2000, cited in http://www.issues2000.org/Celeb/Pat_Buchanan_Immigration.htm. 2002.

Pat Buchanan on Foreign Policy. http://www.issues2000.org/Celeb/Pat_Buchanan_Foreign_Policy.htm. 2002.

Press Release, World Health Organization. http://www.who.int/whr/1996/press.html. 2002.

Table I-38, Air Passenger Travel Departures from the United States to Selected Foreign Countries (Thousands). http://www.bts.gov/btsprod/nts/Ch1web/1-38.htm. 2002.

Terror Attack Expected to Have "Catastrophic" Effect for World Tourism. http://secure.canoe.ca/MoneyRebuild/sept17_tourism-ap.html. 2002.

Text of President Bush's Speech, September 20, 2001. http://www.geocities.com/christymwl/USA_Bush_Speech_9-20-2001.html. 2002.

The NAFTA Scam. http://www.uniteunion.org/reclaim/politicalarchive/nafta/nafta.html. 2002.

Trade Fast Track Agreements. http://www.udarrell.com/fasttrack.html. 2002.

Tuberculosis and Air Travel, Executive Summary. http://www.who.int/gtb/publications/aircraft/summary.html. 2002.

United Nations, Globalization Panel. http://www.unpan1.un.org/intradoc/groups/public/documents/un/unpan001917.pdf. 2002.

INDEX

bomb, 9; Cold War, 4–6, 132; collapse of, 16–18, 35, 58, 110–11, 123, 143; Marshall Plan, 7; NATO, 8; Olympics, 114; Sputnik, 11

Sports, 114–15

Sputnik, 11, 12, 112

"Stagflation," 33

Stalin, Joseph, 6, 7

Stevenson, Adlai, 5

Suez Crisis, 4, 26, 114

Tariffs, xvi, xx, 3, 22, 26, 27, 30, 35, 50, 61, 67, 69, 99, 136, 143, 144; Fordney-McCumber, 22; Hawley-Smoot, 22; NAFTA, 35–37; non-tariff barriers, xvi, 35, 54; Reciprocal Trade Act of 1934, 23, 26, 127

Television, 13, 14, 48–49, 108, 114; development and impact of, 50–52; terrorism, 127–28

Terrorism, 75, 94, 98, 122, 143, 150, 153; *Achille Lauro*, 129. *See also* World Trade Center

Textiles, 26, 39, 54, 67, 75–78, 136, 144, 145; Multi-Fiber Agreement, 77; voluntary export restraints, 80

Thailand, 56

Tiger economies, 56–57

Tourism, 45, 82, 139; disease, 120; foreign currencies, 54–55; globalization of, 71–75; spread of English, 106–7; terrorism, 134; Tiger economies, 56

Transnational corporations (TNCs), xiv, xv–xvii, xx, 17, 34, 49, 61, 62, 146, 151, 153; automobiles, 81; capital flows, 65; criticism of, 40, 111, 139; currency exchange, 50; labor, 94, 152; McDonaldization, 123; NAFTA, 37, 92; Seattle demonstrations, 39; soccer, 115; technology, 43, 52–57, 82; terrorism, 128, 132, 142; tourism, 73–74; WTO, 148

Truman, Harry S., 4, 5, 6, 7, 28, 29, 107; American economic leadership, 41, 151; containment, 8; Korean War, 10; Reciprocal Trade Act, 27

Truman Doctrine, 5, 6, 18, 28

Union of Needletrades, Industrial, and Textile Employees (UNITE), 37

United Nations, 4, 5, 53, 100; English language, 107; ethics of globalization, 151; IPCC, 60; social need, 149–50; tourism, 72, 74; transgenic crops, 71; UNRRA, 6, 66

Vietnam, 46; food, 117; globalization, 14; immigrants, 91, 122

Vietnam War, 14–16, 131

Voluntary export restraints (VER), 76, 80

Wallach, Lori, 148

White, Harry Dexter, 24

Wilson, Pete, 97

Wilson, Woodrow, 1–2

Wooldridge, Adrian, 43

World Bank, xx, 41, 53; antiglobalists, 40; Bretton Woods, 24–25; capital flows, 54; criticism of, 39, 100; globalization, 147–48, 150

World Economic Forum, xiii, 139, 151

World Health Organization (WHO), 117, 118, 119, 121

World Tourism Organization (WTO), 74–75; terrorism, 134

World Trade Center: attack of 1993, 98, 122, 129; attack of 2001, xiii, 74, 127–28, 132–33; and British alliance, 135; fear of air travel, 134

World Trade Organization (WTO), xvi, 54, 95, 123, 142, 150; agriculture, 38–39, 67; arbitration, 144; and China, 15, 69; creation of, 27–28, 35;